Conquer Loneliness

Understand Your Loneliness—and Banish It Forever!

Frank J. Bruno, Ph.D.

Macmillan • USA

Life's Little Keys

Self-Help Strategies for a Happier, Healthier You

ADDITIONAL TITLES

Stop Worrying

Conquer Shyness

Stop Procrastinating

Defeat Depression

Get a Good Night's Sleep

PREFACE

Loneliness.

There it is. It's just a word.

Loneliness.

But it's more than a word. Loneliness is a distressing personal experience. To be lonely is to live in a psychological and emotional wasteland. Oh, there are other people all around. But they might as well be ghosts. You are an invisible presence to them. They don't *see* you or *know* you or seem to really *care*.

What can you do about loneliness?

Can mere words printed on paper actually help?

In the movie *Shadowlands*, the author and scholar C. S. Lewis confronts a poor student who has stolen a book. In their exchange, the student quotes his own father, a village schoolmaster. The impoverished young scholar says, "We read to know we're not alone." If this is true, this book, or almost any book, can help you feel less lonely. As one who has read a fair share of books, I can testify that this is true up to a point.

However, the companionship of a book is transient. Worse, it is synthetic and second hand. You need the companionship of real people—people of flesh and bone—to really overcome personal alienation.

This book is designed to help you do just that. *Conquer Loneliness* will help you understand how emotional isolation is not something that happens to you, but how you bring it on yourself. More, it points out ways that really work, to help you end prolonged loneliness.

I hope you find it to be a practical, useful book.

ACKNOWLEDGMENTS

A number of people have helped me make *Conquer Loneliness* a reality. My thanks are expressed to:

Barbara Gilson, senior editor at Macmillan, for her recognition of the value of the book and for being a supportive and creative editor.

Jennifer Perillo, editor at Macmillan, for her assistance and for her appreciation of the book's themes.

George J. McKeon, artist, for his capturing of key ideas in cartoon form.

Bert Holtje, my agent, for encouraging the development of the book.

My wife, Jeanne, for our many meaningful discussions.

My son, Franklin, for our conversations about language and meaning.

George K. Zaharoupoulos, a true teaching colleague, for his steadfast encouragement of my writing projects.

1 FEELING LONELY IN A CROWD: EXAMINING A STATE OF MIND

You are lonely.

And you are suffering.

You can readily relate to one or several of the following mental or emotional states associated with loneliness:

Isolation

Alienation

Rejection

Feeling misunderstood

Feeling unloved

Depression

Friendlessness

Feeling shut in and/or shut out

Boredom

Restlessness

And, of course, the list could be extended.

What's more, your loneliness isn't superficial. It doesn't go away easily. It's persistent and nagging. It's like a bad cold you can't shake. Or it's like an enemy that follows you around day and night—always there. But it's an enemy that keeps itself out of reach, a vague specter that seems to have no reality at all when you try to come to grips with it. You feel helpless in its presence.

Loneliness is experienced as something that is happening to you, not as something you are doing to yourself. You are its victim. And it is destroying the quality of your life.

Is there any hope?

Is there anything you can do?

I think that the answer to both of these questions is *yes*. I believe that the ideas and suggestions presented in this book will help you to (1) understand the nature of loneliness and (2) find effective ways to overcome it.

Kinds of Loneliness

Think about old Scrooge from Charles Dickens's *A Christmas Carol*. Was he lonely? Of course he was. He treated his employees like worthless dogs, he hated children, he never smiled, he wasn't married, and he treasured money more than life itself. He didn't love anybody. And, of course, nobody loved him back. How could he be anything but lonely? Even though during the day he seemed a proud and aloof man, by night he was like a fearful child, susceptible to the terrors of the ghosts that came to visit him.

Scrooge's story had a happy ending. When he was able to reach out to people, people were there for him. When he changed his attitude, the very fabric of his existence changed. And he overcame his loneliness.

I have introduced the story of Scrooge at this point not to point out the error of his ways, although they are more or less obvious. No, I simply want us to come to grips with the facts of loneliness in some kind of concrete way. And most of us can readily see Scrooge as a lonely man. The question is: What defines loneliness? What common characteristics make for that state we call loneliness?

It will be helpful for us to start with a more or less formal definition of loneliness. That way, as we explore the various byways of loneliness presented in the book, we

will not get completely lost. We will always know what we are talking about.

Loneliness is a negative mental and emotional state characterized principally by feelings of isolation and a lack of meaningful relationships with others. Let's allow this short definition to stand as the core definition of loneliness. It is fairly brief. But it also speaks volumes.

There are different kinds of loneliness. An important distinction can be made between transient loneliness and chronic loneliness. *Transient loneliness* is both brief and passing. It's like a cold wind that appears suddenly out of nowhere and vanishes just as suddenly back into nowhere. It is reactive and situational. You have been invited to a party, and you know only the host and hostess. Other people seem to be friendly and know each other. No one seems to be interested in you. They don't seem to be seeing you as a person. Your host and hostess are busy with others. You feel neglected and rejected. You will almost inevitably experience transient loneliness under these circumstances. Almost any of us would.

By the way, feeling lonely at a party captures the essence of the title of this chapter, "Feeling Lonely in a Crowd." We all know that the mere presence of other people is not a sufficient condition for us to overcome loneliness.

Chronic loneliness is persistent. The root meaning of the word *chronic* is derived from the Greek word for "time." Consequently, chronic loneliness is long-lasting loneliness. It is the kind of loneliness that seems to go on and on, and you wonder if it will ever end. It is corrosive and life destroying. It is likely that if you are motivated to read this book, you suffer to some degree from chronic loneliness. It has many faces and is aggravated by a number of psychological factors. The principal objective of this book is to offer you real help and hope if you suffer from this kind of loneliness.

The distinction between transient and chronic loneliness is not the only way to look at kinds of loneliness. Another way to analyze loneliness is to define the following three categories:

1. Cognitive loneliness

2. Behavioral loneliness

3. Emotional loneliness

Cognitive Loneliness occurs when you have few, if any, people with whom to share some of your more significant thoughts. Olga R. is a full-time homemaker with three children ranging in age from one year to five years. Recently, due to her husband's promotion to a managerial position, the family moved to a new community several hundred miles from more familiar territory. Olga wants to write short stories and novels, and she works at her creative endeavors in off hours. But she would like to talk about the writing process with someone. Her husband comes home from work late and listens politely, but they share no meaningful exchange of ideas. She feels as if she is in a cognitive vacuum. And she is.

≈≈≈ ≈≈≈ ≈≈≈ ≈≈≈ ≈≈≈ ≈≈≈ ≈≈≈ ≈≈≈ ≈≈≈

Dalton O., age sixty-seven, is a retired college professor of mathematics. He and his wife moved to a retirement community. He is a rather introverted man, quiet, and doesn't make friends easily. He likes to discuss abstract ideas revolving around mathematics and philosophy. He enjoyed many such discussions when he worked. His colleagues had similar interests. Now, he says, "There is no one I can talk to about scientific topics that interest me." His wife, although loving, is not really able to help him meet his cognitive needs. And he suffers from cognitive loneliness.

Behavioral Loneliness exists when you lack companions for excursions and activities outside of the home. You want to go see a movie, but there is no one you know who will go with you. Perhaps you go alone, but the pleasure of seeing the movie is greatly diminished. You want to have dinner out. You are forced to go to a family restaurant by yourself. The sight of couples eating and parents fussing with their children aggravates your sense of loneliness. In order to play even a simple card game, with the exception of solitaire, you need at least one other person. When we travel, go to museums, go shopping, set up a garage sale, and so forth, we yearn for at least one other person to share the experience with. Activities and many projects seem to demand companionship. If you find yourself deprived in this area, you tend to suffer from behavioral loneliness.

Emotional Loneliness is the kind of loneliness that takes place when your need for affection is not met. This is the most important and the worst kind of loneliness. Research suggests that we have an inborn need for affection. The experimental psychologist Harry Harlow studied this need in infant Rhesus monkeys and discovered that they fail to thrive if they are deprived of parental love. They show signs that are reminiscent of infantile autism and childhood schizophrenia in human children.

We don't have to look at the behavior of monkeys to convince us that there is an inborn affectional drive, a drive as real and as powerful as the hunger drive. Studies of infants in orphanages in emerging nations have found that the infants often receive quite adequate care in terms of food and medical attention. But they are deprived in terms of the affectional drive. They do not receive the quality of play, attention, and natural interest that is spontaneously given by most parents. Consequently, many of these children show a retarded developmental quotient. They do not sit up, crawl, and walk as soon as children in normal homes. They are prone to sickness and their death rate is above average. This is because even the immune system seems to be compromised by a lack of the proper kind of stimulation and affection. Clinical names such as *hospitalism* and *anaclitic depression* have been attached to their morbid states. However, it would be quite accurate to say that these infants are suffering from emotional loneliness.

You never outgrow your need for affection. You need it as an infant. And you need it as a child, adolescent, and adult. You need it, if not every day, on a fairly regular basis. You need affection the way you need food and water. Sarah E. is married to a cold, unloving man. They have been married for eight years and have two children. For various reasons she is enduring the marriage, and maybe she should not. But she is a traditional woman and her religion frowns on divorce. And there is a lot of family pressure, particularly from her mother, to continue the marriage. And Sarah tries. She is a good cook, a loving mother, and wants to be a responsive sexual partner.

But her husband just seems to take everything for granted and has very little to say. He seldom smiles. He almost never volunteers an anecdote associated with his work. Her husband doesn't meet her affectional needs. And they are not being met elsewhere. (Her mother is overcontrolling and emotionally remote.) Sarah hasn't defined it this way, but she is suffering from emotional loneliness.

Solitude

It is important to realize that solitude can be quite different from loneliness. A state of solitude exists when you are alone. It is the absence of other people. There are times to seek solitude. A duration spent in solitude can be creative and life enhancing, and you may not suffer from loneliness at all.

A basic distinction can be made between voluntary solitude and involuntary solitude. *Voluntary solitude* is solitude of your own choosing. It is an experience you look forward to. It provides you with a "time out" from other people, from the world and its concerns. It is an opportunity to think, to lick your psychological wounds, to write, to paint, to listen to your favorite music, to meditate, and so forth.

Involuntary solitude, of the other hand, is not of your own choosing. It is thrust upon you. You find yourself isolated from others at a time when you crave human contact. If involuntary solitude goes on too long, it can be a debilitating experience. And it is this kind of solitude that induces loneliness.

In 1938 the explorer Admiral Richard E. Byrd spent five months without companionship during the Antarctic night. He lived in a relatively small plywood building that he called a "shack," and collected meteorological data. He wrote about his experiences in his book *Alone*. His only contact with others occurred several minutes a week when he listened to a voice radio message from Little America, the base camp located a few hundred miles to the north. He responded in Morse code. He is very clear in the book that he sought this experience, that he looked forward to it, and that he was interested in what he could learn from it.

In the entire book Byrd refers to feeling lonely only once. This lasted for a brief period. It was transient, and he coped with it by keeping busy and sticking to a structured daily plan. He certainly did not suffer from life-corroding chronic loneliness. Why? First, as indicated earlier, Byrd's variety of voluntary solitude can be life enhancing. Second, he had a loving wife and affectionate children. He had a solid marriage to return to. His confidence in an eventual happy reunion sustained him and nurtured his emotional life.

So don't confuse solitude with loneliness. In your fight against loneliness, there are times when you will want to use solitude in a creative way.

What This Book Can Do For You

Conquer Loneliness takes the position that loneliness is not something that happens to you, but something that you do to yourself. I know it doesn't feel that way. It feels like you are its victim.

However, a difference needs to be drawn between being an actual victim and playing the social role of Victim. (Notice that the social role of Victim is capitalized. This is to distinguish it from being an actual victim, in which circumstances quite beyond your control create both physical and emotional disasters.) In the case of the Victim role, you *add* to a sad state of affairs with either a maladaptive attitude or somewhat irrational thoughts. The Victim's role also is reinforced by a search for pity from others. When pity is obtained, the Victim's role is reinforced and tends to become an entrenched pattern.

Actual victims have no control over circumstances. Things just happen. Airplanes crash, buildings burn, people are trapped in the rubble produced by an earthquake, recessions and depressions happen, civil wars erupt, and so forth. On the other hand, persons playing the Victim's role *do* have control over circumstances. They have *a lot of power*. But they tend to *perceive* the locus of control outside of themselves when it is actually within.

This book will help you to see that in the vast majority of cases when you feel lonely you are not an actual victim. The way you are playing your psychological cards is making you into a Victim. You can play your cards differently, and overcome loneliness.

A key concept in this book may be termed *strategic intervention*. Strategic intervention refers to relatively straightforward, common sense things you can do to escape from loneliness. One of the assumptions of strategic intervention is that small changes can produce big results. Imagine that you are taking a car trip through California. At a certain choice point in the vicinity of Los Angeles, you turn your wheels to the right, and head north. Eventually you wind up in San Francisco. Now imagine going back to the choice point. You turn your wheels to the left and head south. Eventually you find yourself in San Diego. How long did it take to make the turn? A minute? Less? Notice that a *small* effort produce a very large result. So it is in the realm of psychology. Small steps in the right direction can eventually produce large, beneficial results.

This book presents you with numerous practical, self-directed coping strategies that offer genuine hope, strategies that will really help you give up the Victim's role and overcome chronic loneliness.

You will not have to change your basic personality in order to overcome loneliness. That is one of the advantages of the strategic approach. It does not see you as a flawed person who must be "fixed." On the contrary, you are all right just the way you are. However, you probably can learn better coping skills, skills that will bring you closer to people and help you obtain a larger share of positive attention and recognition than you are presently obtaining.

Finally, it is essential to understand that overcoming loneliness is a lifelong learning process. It isn't something you achieve once at a certain point in your life. Unfortunately, you can't just rest on your oars and say, "That's it. I can relax now. I'm not lonely any more." You must *nurture* your human relationships just as you must water your plants on a regular basis. However, just as plant lovers enjoy taking care of their plants, people who both like and love others enjoy exercising the skills that overcome loneliness. So think of overcoming loneliness as a joyful process.

The Last Word

More than two thousand years ago the philosopher Aristotle said, "No one would choose a friendless existence on condition of having all the other things in the world." Think of it. Nothing, *nothing at all*, is more important than meaningful relationships with other people. This book is dedicated to helping you achieve this end: A life enriched by love and friendship, a life in which you have acquired the skills to overcome loneliness.

Key Points to Remember

🖛 Loneliness is a negative mental and emotional state characterized principally by feelings of isolation and a lack of meaningful relationships with others.

🖛 Transient loneliness is both brief and passing.

🖛 Chronic loneliness is persistent and long lasting.

🖛 Cognitive loneliness occurs when you have few if any people to share some of your more significant thoughts with.

🖛 Behavioral loneliness exists when you lack companions for excursions and activities outside of the home.

🖛 Emotional loneliness is the kind of loneliness that takes place when your need for affection is not met.

🖛 A state of solitude exists when you are alone. It is the absence of other people.

🖛 Voluntary solitude is solitude of your own choosing. It is often a condition for positive experiences.

□━ Involuntary solitude is not of your own choosing. It is this kind of solitude that induces loneliness.

□━ This book presents you with numerous practical, self-directed coping strategies that offer genuine hope, strategies that will really help you give up the social role of Victim and overcome chronic loneliness.

2 MEETING PEOPLE: MAKING CONTACT

The problem of overcoming loneliness is not the same as the problem of meeting people. You can meet a lot of people, you can have numerous acquaintances who aren't really friends, and you can have a series of dates with people you do not find sufficiently attractive. And you can still be lonely.

Nonetheless, contacts with other people are *necessary* in order to overcome loneliness. Contacts in and of themselves just aren't *sufficient*. Most of the chapters in this book are dedicated to the "sufficient" aspect of human relationships. They assume that you *do* have social contacts, but that they must be nurtured and converted into meaningful relationships. However, this chapter takes a different tack. It is directed to those of you who believe that a large part of your loneliness problem could be solved by meeting the right person or persons.

Perhaps you are "a stranger in a strange land." You have just moved into a new town or city. Or it is possible that you live where you have always lived, and you just don't feel that you've met the person or persons you want to meet. Maybe you are single and looking for a partner. No matter the case, the suggestions in this chapter may prove helpful in meeting people.

No particular distinction is made in the following material between meeting a potential partner and meeting potential friends. The kinds of things you need to do and the sorts of places you need to go to make social contacts are essentially similar. And, remember, the ideal partner *is* a friend.

Making Contact

Meeting people revolves around the art of making contacts. It is not enough to meet people. One must meet the right person in the right way. As already indicated, the skills involved in forming rewarding human relationships will be covered in following chapters. The strategies presented in this section focus only on making initial connections with others.

OBVIOUS AVENUES

Don't Overlook Obvious Avenues of Contact. The simple truth is that most people make their initial contacts with others in rather obvious ways. We meet people on the job, through other friends, through family, and at school. These avenues, in fact, are our principal sources of friends and partners.

Cameron S. wanted to meet someone he could fall in love with and marry. His grandmother, who worked part time as a sales clerk at a department store, told him that she had met a "nice" young woman named Vicky at work and could arrange an introduction. Cameron discounted his grandmother's suggestion. The grandmother persisted. Finally Cameron reluctantly agreed to meet the other person. Cameron and Vicky dated, clicked, got engaged, and now are married. This is not an unusual story. In fact various versions of it are very common. The grandmother served as a matchmaker, a traditional and honorable role.

MEETING CUTE

Don't Insist on Meeting Cute. In books on writing for would-be romance authors, standard advice is to arrange for the couple to "meet cute." Examples include meeting on a cruise, as the result of an auto accident, with secret identities, and so forth. An example of meeting cute is provided by the classical film It Happened One Night. The Clark Gable character is hired by a rich father to track down and bring back his runaway daughter, played by Claudette Colbert. When Gable finds Colbert in a remote place, sparks fly. Strangers to each other, they are forced to spend a night in a motel together. Subsequently they have a series of humorous adventures. They overcome their initial hostility and fall in love. The picture was made in 1934, and swept the Academy Awards. Now, more than sixty years later, movie romances still have couples meeting cute. For example, Sleepless in Seattle and Forget Paris make use of this device.

It is easy to be subconsciously influenced by the movie formula. You meet someone and you ask yourself, "Did we meet cute?" If the answer is *no*, you may think that a more magical meeting with a different person is fated in your future. Instead, you need to be a realist. *How* you meet someone means very little. If you meet in an ordinary way, through work or family, be satisfied. Focus on the *person*, not the way in which you have met.

SELECTED PLACES

Become a Regular Visitor to Places That Are Likely to Attract Persons With Values and Interests in Common With Yours. Two of the key words above are values and interests. As already noted, in order to overcome loneliness, it is not enough to make contact with people. The psychological opposite of loneliness is closeness, and you can't have closeness with people who have outlooks that are at great variance to your own. On the other hand, it is easy to strike up a conversation, and eventually develop a friendship, with persons who share your values and interests. You might meet such people at bookstores, galleries, museums, libraries, and antique stores, for example.

Henrietta F. says, "I met one of my best friends, Beth, at a local bookstore about three years ago. I used to stop in to browse at least once a week. Several times I noticed a particular other woman in the store. Sometimes we stood next to each other, but never spoke. I couldn't help but notice that her tastes in reading were similar to mine. Although we both bought paperback romances, I noticed that from time to time she also purchased an inexpensive edition of a classic such as *Of Human Bondage* or *Anna Karenina*.

"One day I gathered my courage and decided to introduce myself. I steeled myself for a put-off. Instead, I received a warm response. She was glad I had spoken to her, wanted to talk to me several times in the past, and hesitated to do so, thinking she might offend me.

"We went to a nearby family restaurant for coffee, talked almost an hour, and discovered that we were both married, lived in the same suburb, and had teenage children. What's more important, we both loved to read the same kind of books. Since that first visit, Beth and I formed a real bond of mutual respect and affection."

Carl V. says, "I met my fiancée at an art gallery. A frequent drop-in, on two different occasions I saw an attractive woman spending some time studying a painting of the ocean at midnight by a local painter. It was a canvas that I liked very much. The third time I saw her, I summoned up a little bit of nerve, stood near her, took a deep breath, and said, 'I too admire that painting.'

"She turned to me, hesitated a moment, and then smiled. She said, 'Isn't it beautiful? There's something about it that's really special.'

"We chatted, got acquainted, and eventually exchanged telephone numbers. Nothing could have been more natural, once the ice was broken."

CLUBS

Join a Club. Clubs are automatic magnets for people with similar values and interests. And most clubs are on the lookout for new members. If you will open either the Yellow Pages or the Advertising Directory of your telephone book, you will find the headings "Clubs" and "Organizations." Just a partial listing includes: (1) square dance clubs; (2) senior citizen organizations; (3) bowling leagues; (4) writer's clubs; (5) women's clubs; (6) fraternal organizations; (7) the American Legion and the Veterans of Foreign Wars; and (8) Parents Without Partners.

Rhonda N., married to Jesse, says, "About seven years ago we were strangers in town. Jesse had been transferred here with his company, and we didn't know a soul. We joined a square dance club. Now our best friends are people in the club. We've seen each other through children and illnesses, through some good times and some bad times. It's much more than a dancing club. It's a kind of second family."

Frazer O. says, "I've always wanted to write novels as an avocation. I'm a full-time attorney. None of my friends or family seemed to take my aspirations very seriously. I joined a local writer's club and met people with dreams and ambitions that are similar to mine. They encourage me and I encourage them. I've become very friendly with several people in the club. And I'm doing sustained work on a novel."

CLASSES

Take a Class. Classes are offered to adults by community colleges, extension divisions of universities, city recreational departments, and so forth. You can take classes in almost anything and everything ranging from psychology to tennis, from history to music, from sewing to public speaking. Evening classes in particular are a great way to meet people because there is usually a fifteen- or twenty-minute break between two sessions. During these break periods it is customary for students to mix, to chat, and to get acquainted. It is an open invitation to get to know people. No one will wonder why you are introducing yourself or expressing an idea.

COMMUNITY ACTIVITY

Become Active in Your Community. If you are a parent, get involved in the PTA. If you are a property owner, go to planning commission and city council meetings. If you can spare the time, join the volunteer corps at your local hospital. Other possibilities include volunteer work as a library aide or as a classroom assistant at a grammar school. These are all constructive activities, and they are also excellent ways to get out into the world and meet people.

CHURCH MEMBERSHIP

Consider Becoming a Church Member. Let's assume that you genuinely identify with a particular religious viewpoint. You don't deny the teachings of your church, but you have drifted away. It might be time to consider becoming a church member. Membership, with real conviction, in a church will provide you with emotional satisfaction and simultaneously help you to satisfy your search for meaning in life. On the secular side, dinners and other social events sponsored by the church provide a practical way to meet people with values that are likely to be similar to your own.

PEOPLE EVERYWHERE

Talk to a Lot of People. People are everywhere. You will see the same ones regularly at your neighborhood coffee shop, drug store, gas station, beauty or barber shop, health food store, bank, clothing store, supermarket, and so forth. One is reminded of a well-known line from "The Rime of the Ancient Mariner" by Samuel Taylor Coleridge: "Water, water everywhere! And not a drop to drink." If you are in a state of social isolation, you feel as if there are people, people everywhere, but not a friend in sight.

You need to make contacts with people before you can overcome social isolation, before you can convert strangers into friends. Consequently you need to talk to these people that are everywhere. You need to strike up conversations. Any little excuse to speak will do. If you are waiting to pick up a prescription, you can make a comment related to health. If you are buying clothes, you can comment on style or ask someone near you for an opinion concerning the color of a particular item you are considering. If you are waiting in a long line, you can either comment on the length of the line or the weather. Very seldom, almost never, will you get a hostile response. On the contrary, more often than not, people welcome being spoken too. If a given individual does not, simply discontinue your efforts with that person.

If you are friendly and speak to a lot of people, you will find that you click with some of them. And a contact providing a potential for a friendship has been established.

SOCIAL EVENTS

Go to Every Social Event to Which You Are Invited. If you are invited to a wedding, a school reunion, a picnic, a birthday party, a niece's high school graduation, or similar function, go. You need to get out into the world, to mix with others, in order to overcome social isolation. You need to be where the people are. Willie Sutton, a bank robber, was once asked, "Why do you rob banks?" He answered, "Because that's where the money is." Ridiculous, but true. A bank is where the money is. And you have to go where the people are. And they are present at social events.

DATING SERVICES

Employ a Dating Service. In larger communities you will find professional dating services. Some of these provide videotapes of persons you might consider dating. You, of course, also provide a videotape of yourself. This gives you an opportunity to screen each other, to see if you like the person's appearance and surface personality before you even date. Also, the dating service provides background information on the other's career, age, interests, values, hobbies, and so forth. Again, you need to proceed with some degree of caution. People can, and sometimes do, lie on questionnaires. On the other hand, dating services sometimes really do provide a first contact that leads

. . . and my interests include bug-catching, waste removal and linoleum.

to a long-term relationship. Fees can be quite high, so be prepared to part with some cash. A dating service essentially serves the same function as the old-fashioned matchmaker.

PERSONAL ADS

Consider Responding to or Placing a Personal Ad. Open any newspaper and turn to the classified section. You will find quite a few personal ads. Although some are just looking for friendships, the majority are seeking to make a love connection. Respond to one of the ads. Or take out your own ad. However, you need to use some common sense and proceed with caution. There is more about this in the section headed "Be Aware."

BARS AND PUBS

If You Have No Tendency to Abuse Alcohol, Become a Regular Visitor to a Local Bar or Pub. Duffy's Tavern was a popular radio program in the 1940s. Cheers, running for many years on television, was a similar production. Both of these shows presented a bar as a principal location. At the bar, people got to know each other, shared their personal problems, laughed and cried together, and became a kind of self-selected family. A bar can serve this function, and does, for many people.

The principal drawback, of course, is the problem of alcohol abuse. If you can take or leave alcohol, then a bar can be a practical way to meet people. However, if you are likely to abuse alcohol, you need to stay away from bars.

It should be noted, however, that there are other kinds of bars. There are fruit and vegetable juice bars in health clubs. And coffee bars are becoming increasingly popular. An establishment near my home calls itself a "juice and java" bar.

PART-TIME WORK

If You Are a Full-Time Homemaker, Get a Part-Time Outside Job. The main exception to this suggestion is if you have one or two infants or toddlers, and you feel that it is impossible to break away. Even then, you might be able to work something out that allows for limited day care. In any event, if at all possible, don't make homemaking your one and only vocation.

If you have a marketable skill, you are in a very desirable position. But even if you don't, there is a lot of part-time work available. Often, on-the-job training is available for semiskilled work. Examples include employment as a receptionist, host or hostess, food server, bank teller, and sales clerk.

If you stay in your home too many hours, you are not only in social isolation, you are also in a state of sensory deprivation. *Sensory deprivation* is characterized by insufficient changes in stimulation to the eyes, the ears, and your other sense organs. A large body of evidence in experimental psychology suggests that social isolation and sensory deprivation have an adverse impact on mental health.

You are very likely to meet interesting people on almost any job. Why? Because a lot of people, even superficially ordinary people, are often fascinating and complex if you get to know them a little, if you get below the surface.

It is not at all difficult to find part-time work. You will find plenty of ads in the classified section of your newspaper. Or you can sign up with an agency that specializes in placing temporary workers.

SUPPORT GROUP

If You Have a Specific Personal Problem, Consider Joining a Support Group. Not only will a group help you deal with your problem, you are quite likely to form some friendships. Well-known groups include Alcoholics Anonymous (AA), Al-Anon, Neurotics Anonymous (NA), Take Off Pounds Sensibly (TOPS) and Overeaters Anonymous (OA), Tough Love, and Parents Without Partners. You will find names and phone numbers listed in your telephone directory. You can also obtain information from a reference librarian or your local mental health association.

One of the principal advantages of support groups is that there are no professional fees to pay. There are no contracts to sign, and you are in control of your participation.

Read the entertaining mystery novels about Matt Scudder, private eye, by Lawrence Block for an example of how a support group (in this case, AA) can help a person keep functioning. Again, you get two-in-one with a support group: social contacts plus emotional support. These groups can be an important resource in successfully overcoming loneliness.

ONLINE SERVICES

Consider Subscribing to an Online Service. Online services provide a way to make contacts with many people, both in and out of the United States. Examples of online services include America Online, CompuServe, Interpath, and Novalink. Online services also provide access to the Internet. There are presently millions of subscribers to these services, and the number is growing.

In order to use online services, you need to own, or have access to, an appropriate computer, essential software, and a modem. The *modem* allows you to use telephone lines to connect with other computers with modems. If you feel threatened by computers and unfamiliar terms, be assured that a local computer store can readily set you up and install all the required software. One of the stores near my home offers a short course on how to use the Internet for a modest fee.

The key point to be made is that an online service allows you to enter a "chat" mode. Chatting is accomplished by electronic mail (E-mail), a virtually instantaneous form of communication. There are "public rooms" where you can meet people. If a particular person interests you, you can enter a "private room" and chat only with each other. The chat mode in and of itself is a way to meet interesting people at a cognitive level and overcome loneliness.

On the other hand, if a contact seems particularly promising, you can exchange photographs with the other person, make direct telephone calls, and arrange face-to-face meeting times. And, yes, there *are* cases of persons who have found romance and formed long-term relationships, including marriage, via initial contacts made using an online service.

STRANGERS

Remember That It's OK for Grown-Ups to Talk to Strangers. When you were a child, your parents told you, "Never talk to strangers." And the impression carries over to adulthood. The author Harold Robbins titled his first novel Never Love a Stranger. A mistrust of the newcomer, the outsider, the unknown person is an emotional conditioned reflex that burdens many of us. However, most friends and lovers were once strangers. The barrier must be overcome. Don't listen only to the warning from your child self. You are all grown up now. And it is OK to talk to a stranger.

BE AWARE

Be Aware, Be Careful, and Be Realistic. Yes, give yourself permission to talk to strangers. However, having said this, do be aware of potential risks. Without becoming excessively paranoid, it is prudent to remind yourself that not everyone can be trusted, that not everything can be taken at face value.

Sociopaths, persons with no conscience and an absence of guilt feelings, may use and abuse personal ads, dating services, and online services. They are likely to prey on lonely persons. Before you get deeply involved with someone else, do a reality check. Get as much collateral information about the person as you can. Make an effort to get to know the individual's friends and family.

The Last Word

A central theme is this chapter has been that in order to meet people you must reach out, you must become an *active agent.* You can't just be passive and expect people to find you. You must move toward them. Yes, some will draw away or display a lack of interest. You *do* have be prepared for the occasional rejection. But, on the whole, you will find that people are pleased when you take the first step. It takes the burden of initiating contact off of them, and they need only respond if they are interested. And, more often than not, they are.

It takes a bit of audacity to make the first contact with another person. However, an observation made about five hundred years ago by the Dutch scholar Desiderius Erasmus is worth remembering. He said, "Fortune favors the audacious."

Key Points to Remember

☐— Contacts with other people are *necessary* in order to overcome loneliness. However, contacts in and of themselves aren't *sufficient.*

☐— This chapter was directed to you if you believe that a large part of your loneliness problem can solved by meeting the right person or persons.

☐— No particular distinction was made in this chapter between meeting a potential partner and meeting potential friends. The ideal partner *is* a friend.

☐— Don't overlook obvious avenues of contact.

☐— Don't insist on meeting cute.

- Become a regular visitor to bookstores, galleries, museums, libraries, antique stores, or other places that are likely to attract persons with values and interests in common with yours.

- Join a club.

- Take a class.

- Become active in your community.

- Consider becoming a church member.

- Talk to a lot of people.

- Go to every social event that you are invited to.

- If you have no tendency to abuse alcohol, become a regular visitor to a local bar or pub.

- Consider responding to or placing a personal ad.

- Employ a dating service.

- If you are a full-time homemaker, get a part-time outside job.

- If you have a specific personal problem such as alcoholism or obesity, consider joining a support group.

- Explore the possibility of subscribing to an online service.

- Remember that it's OK for grown-ups to talk to strangers.

- Be aware, be careful, and be realistic.

3 THE NEED FOR AFFECTION: ARE YOU GETTING YOUR STROKES?

Antonia is a seventeen-month-old infant. Her arms remind you of breadsticks. Her sad, large eyes gaze steadily at nothing, lacking focus. She is prone to infections and is a sickly child. Although her chronological age is, as indicated, seventeen months, her developmental quotient, a measure of her motor abilities and general responsiveness, is only fourteen months.

What is wrong with Antonia? Is she suffering from a birth defect? Does she have a maladaptive food absorption problem such as phenylketonuria (PKU)? Does she have Down's syndrome? No, she has none of the problems indicated.

She was a healthy, robust newborn, and should have developed normally. However, Antonia's mother, a single woman, died when the infant was only two months old. No family accepted Antonia, and she is one of more than forty infants in an orphanage in a developing country. Although it appears that Antonia *does* receive an adequate amount of protein and reasonably good basic health care, she is failing to thrive. A formal term for her condition is *hospitalism*.

Antonia has developmental problems not because of physical neglect, but because of emotional neglect. Her need for affection is not being met, and Antonia is demonstrating the adverse effects of the lack. No one really cares if she lives or dies. Antonia is bonded to no one. She does not have the love of a parent, and her whole being is withering as a result. She needs, but is not receiving, emotional nurturing in the same way that a plant needs the nurture of water and sunshine.

It is not too far-fetched to suggest that each and every one of us carries within us every day of our lives an inner child that cries out for affection.

Children in orphanages, particularly in understaffed orphanages in developing nations, were found to suffer from hospitalism by the researcher R. A. Spitz. Supporting Spitz's observations, Harry Harlow, a former president of the American Psychological Association, found that if infant monkeys are raised as social isolates and deprived of parental love, they too will fail to thrive just like human infants.

You and I need affection in order to maintain a sense of well being. We need it as surely as we need food and water. Harlow's research strongly indicated that the need for affection is an inborn one, that it is not derived from an association with hunger and thirst. An infant does not develop an emotional bond with a parent because a parent is a food source. Instead, the infant becomes attached because being loved makes one feel secure and worthwhile, at any age.

Stroke Hunger

The psychiatrist Eric Berne was the principal founder of a personality theory known as transactional analysis. *Transactional analysis* is also a method of therapy, and it has spawned such well-known books as Berne's own *Games People Play* and the psychiatrist Thomas Harris's *I'm OK, You're OK*. According to Berne, the principal reason that people engage in *transactions*, verbal and emotional exchanges, is to obtain strokes.

A *stroke* in transactional analysis is a unit of recognition. This unit is the principal token of both human love and affection. (In transactional analysis, love is seen as a kind of affection. It is simply a very powerful form of affection.) The word *stroke* is derived from the stroking

behavior we see among primates—and also among human beings. Stroking behavior includes hugging, cuddling, embracing, snuggling, patting, squeezing, and affectionate touching in general. In the case of highly conscious organisms such as human beings, strokes can also be obtained at a verbal level. Praise, compliments, a kind word, a friendly "Hello," and a thank-you note are all examples of such strokes.

The basic notion is that we need strokes in order to thrive at any age. Obtaining a sufficient number of strokes on a fairly regular basis is a principal way to conquer loneliness. Deprived of strokes, we will be plunged into emotional isolation.

Berne developed a concept called *stroke hunger*. If you are in a state of stroke hunger you will feel cut off from others, shut out of the ongoing stream of life. You will feel like an outsider—as if there is a glass barrier between you and others. And this will be the case no matter how physically close they are to you. This is so true that a person can easily feel lonely even during a sexual encounter if he or she feels used or taken for granted.

Obtaining Strokes

Obtaining strokes is an art. Some people are very good at eliciting stroking behavior from others. On the other hand, as already indicated, if you lack the ability to obtain strokes, you will find yourself in a state of emotional isolation. And you will be lonely.

The self-directed strategies that follow will help you overcome a stroke hunger. They will provide you with practical ways to meet your ongoing need for affection.

EARNING STROKES

Think in Terms of Earning Strokes. A basic distinction is the one between unconditional and conditional strokes. An *unconditional stroke* is one that is spontaneously given. It does not have to be earned. Kristine is a much-loved child. Four years old with no siblings, she is the sunshine of her parents' life. They hug her and kiss her and pay her little compliments at odd times just because they feel like it. To them, she is so special that she doesn't have to *do* anything but just exist in order to elicit strokes.

A *conditional stroke* is one that must be earned. If we do *this*, then we can get *that*. Lester, age nine, has parents who love him—or at least think they do. They are both busy professional persons. Lester's father is a surgeon; his mother is an attorney. Lester is a good boy—a "little angel." He has already learned that in order to obtain strokes from his parents, he has to toe the line. As negative as this sounds, it is the main way in which families have socialized their young throughout the ages.

Although it *would* be better for Lester's development if he got at least a few unconditional strokes, the truth is the he *is* thriving. He is *not* in a stroke vacuum because he has learned to earn strokes.

Look at it this way. In this world we seldom get something for nothing. Common sense says there's no such thing as a free lunch. As adults, it would be nice if we received strokes from other people just because we exist. But it seldom happens.

Let's assume that you are married. You would like your spouse to be more attentive, more affectionate. You recall how in the early days of your relationship and during your honeymoon, it seemed that he or she loved you just because you were you. You had to do very little, or nothing, to get stroked. Now, a few years down the road, everything has changed.

One of the things that has changed is that you have adapted to each other to some extent. The other person is not as exciting to you as he or she once was. Another important change is that you have formed expectations. You *do* expect your spouse to live up to certain responsibilities. If he or she lets you down, you are likely to turn a cold shoulder and withhold strokes. Your partner almost certainly follows a similar pattern. All of this is normal and *as it should be*—even if we don't like it much.

So if you want to be stroked by your partner, live up to your responsibilities. If it's your job to cook the meals, serve well-prepared nutritious ones. If you alternate cooking assignments, on your day take an interest and do a good job. If you have a regular chore, do it with a smile, and promptly. If you have a task to do that will please your partner when accomplished, do it with a positive attitude. These kinds of behaviors are the sort that are most likely to earn you strokes in the form of praise, a hug, a kiss, a smile, and so forth.

The statements made in connection with a spouse also apply to friends. If you do someone a good turn, you are likely to receive a stroke in return.

I have described above what Berne called the *stroke economy*. The stroke economy is our tendency to give and withhold strokes on a conditional basis just as we give and withhold money on a conditional basis. Don't resist the stroke economy. You can say, "I want to be loved just because I'm *me*, not because of what I do." You can repeat this all you want. But, in the end, the stroke economy is bound to prevail. Partners and friends *will* stroke you if you have strokes coming. And, conversely, they *will* withhold strokes if you don't live up to their expectations. *And you will do the same.*

So *do* think in terms of earning strokes. And make your peace with this idea.

LOVELESS PERSONS

Don't Try to Get Strokes from a Stone-Hearted Person. A song that was popular some years ago used the phrase *heart of stone*. A person with a heart of stone is a loveless person. He or she has little or no genuine affection to give. Often such people have narcissistic personalities. They are absorbed in themselves. They can take no real joy in either your presence or your accomplishments.

Perhaps you objected to the earlier principle that you should think in terms of earning strokes, thinking, "Some people won't stroke you no matter what you do." And you are right.

You can't earn strokes from an individual with a narcissistic personality because they *won't pay off their debt to you.*

What is the answer? Don't keep trying. Don't attempt to get strokes from a stone-hearted person. It's amazing how some of us will try and try and try.

Even an experimental rat shows a certain amount of rational behavior in a no-win situation. Faced with lever 1 that no longer gives food when pressed, it switches to lever 2, one that *does* give food. You have to do something similar. Don't waste your time trying to obtain strokes from a person that just won't stroke you.

What if you are married to such a person? This is one of the reasons that couples eventually divorce. Often Person 1 is very affectionate and demonstrative. Person 2 is unwilling or unable to reciprocate. Person 1 at some point may be sufficiently distressed to take active steps to terminate the marriage.

OUTSIDE OF THE HOME

Realize That Sometimes It's OK to Go Outside of the Home or a Marriage in Order to Obtain Strokes. Again, let's assume that you are married. What if your partner is an "in-between?" He or she is not particularly demonstrative or affectionate. On the other hand, he or she *does* sometimes stroke you. You are somewhat stroke deprived, but you are not *completely* starved for affection. It's just that your marriage doesn't adequately meet your need. You don't want to break up your union. Your partner has a number of good points. And there are practical reasons to stay together. There are financial obligations and children to raise. You are staying with your partner on the principle that "a half a loaf is better than none." You're half in love and half out of love. What should you do?

Use the self-directed strategy indicated above. It's OK to seek strokes from people other than your partner. *Any* form of positive recognition is subconsciously interpreted as a sign of affection. So if you have compatible social contacts in the form of acquaintances, coworkers, and friends, you will obtain your share of strokes. Use the strategies listed in chapter 2 in order to increase your number of social contacts.

Don't expect the relationship with your partner to be everything, to satisfy *all* of your need for affection.

ASK AND YOU SHALL RECEIVE

Ask for Strokes. It has been said "Ask and you shall receive." And this is true of strokes. If you want a token of affection, it makes sense to solicit it.

Agnes S. was one of my counseling clients. She had once worked as a legal secretary, but was now a full-time homemaker and the mother of five children. One of her main complaints was that her husband ignored occasions that were special to her. She said, "I never forget his birthday or Father's Day. I always cook him a special meal, give him a card, and have a wrapped present. He basks in the attention. He laps it up. But when it comes to *my* birthday or Mother's Day or our wedding anniversary, I don't even get a greeting card. I never get a gift, and I mean *never*. Not even on Christmas day." Her eyes filled with tears. "And it hurts."

I asked her, "And what do you do when he forgets to get you a card or otherwise ignores a special day?"

She seemed genuinely puzzled by my question. "Why, nothing. I just let it go with a brave smile. I guess I act chipper, as if nothing has happened."

"Then you're sending him the wrong messages. Tell him you would like a card and a gift on special days."

"They wouldn't mean anything if I had to ask for them."

"Then you're expecting him to be a mind reader." "You're feeling hurt and bearing a grudge against him without giving him half a chance. Maybe he *really* thinks there's nothing wrong, that you don't care about getting cards and gifts."

"How could he?"

"You'd be surprised." Then I said, "Look. Give the guy a break. *Ask* for what you want. Explain why certain signs of his love are important to you."

Agnes took my advice. It turned out that her husband was more than willing to be accommodating. She had been giving him the wrong kind of behavioral feedback, expecting him to be "sensitive" and translate her bright smile into the opposite message: "I am hurt." This was asking just a little too much of a fairly ordinary man.

Now she gets her cards and gifts and realizes that they *are* genuine strokes. After all, he *does* love her enough to respond to her request.

There is nothing wrong with saying at certain times, "I'd like a hug." Or, "How about a kiss?" Or, "Rub my back." If the other person responds willingly, the stroke you receive is genuine.

Ask for strokes. There is a more than fifty-fifty chance you will receive them.

NEGATIVE STROKES

Don't Become Addicted to Negative Strokes. A negative stroke, like strokes in general, is a unit of recognition. However, a negative stroke is painful, at either a bodily or an emotional level. Examples of negative strokes include slaps, shoving, arm twisting, insults, harsh criticisms, and name calling. These actions belong to the related categories of physical and verbal abuse.

Why would anyone become addicted to negative strokes? The answer is that the human need for recognition of some kind is so great that in the absence of positive strokes, persons will sometimes seek negative ones. Masochism, in which psychological pleasure is extracted from pain, provides evidence in favor of the general idea that if one is starved for strokes, negative ones will be sought. Negative strokes are perceived subconsciously as a kind of affection, and there is the illusion that emotional isolation has been overcome.

An intimate relationship in which one person is dominated by the other one is called *sadomasochistic*. The sadomasochistic elements need not be physical in nature. They can be emotional. If another person uses and abuses you in any way, and you are addicted to the relationship, then the relationship has sadomasochistic elements.

A sadomasochistic relationship is not restricted to partners. It can also apply to friendships. Margaret G. says, "For three years my best friend was Patricia. We did everything together. I was crazy about her as a person. She was everything I wasn't: slim, pretty, witty, and self-confident. And she applied a lot of her wit in my direction in the form of clever criticism and teasing hostility. Little by little I began to feel that I was her emotional slave. She pulled my string and I jerked. I was always trying to please her. But I somehow saw even her hostility as a strange kind of affection.

"I eventually recognized that I was constantly being taken advantage of. I tried to talk things over with Patricia, but to no avail. She would make a witty remark, discount my concerns, and I'd be back in a submissive, defeated position. I realized that the relationship was giving me a kind of fake closeness, not real warmth. Thank goodness I eventually had the strength to break it off."

FOOD AND STROKES

If You Have a Tendency to be Overweight, Don't Stroke Yourself With Food. When you are lonely you are in a state of stroke hunger. Food is associated with love. After all, our parents fed us and they loved us. Also, when we visit someone's home, food is often offered. Food is a sign that the other person is pleased to see you. Consequently, we associate food with affection, with being liked. It is no wonder that at the subconscious level food is often perceived as having stroke value.

Samantha F., a single woman, says, "Whenever I was by myself in my apartment and feeling lonely, the first thing I thought about was food. I would be sitting there in the evening watching television. I had had a good dinner. But around 9 o'clock I would get a craving for food, and I would start snacking. I ate potato chips, ice cream, cold chicken legs, leftover stew, chocolate chip cookies— anything I had around. And nothing satisfied me. But I kept eating. I was about forty pounds overweight, felt unattractive to men, and this made me feel even lonelier.

"I began going to Overeaters Anonymous and learned that I was using food as a substitute for affection. I remember getting the insight, 'I'm looking for love in all the wrong places.' I realized that I was looking for love and affection in the food. But the truth was *there was no love in the food*. No wonder nothing satisfied me. I

determined to look for ways to satisfy my emotional needs in more constructive, realistic ways. And I was able to do it."

STROKING YOURSELF

Learn to Stroke Yourself. You have heard the phrase *your own best friend.* Be your own best friend and learn to stroke yourself. When you have a little success, give yourself a small reward. The reward itself depends on your individual personality. One person will take some time out to read a novel. Another person will go see a movie. Still another person will buy something to wear. It all depends on you. But give yourself the tokens of affection generously when you feel that you really have them coming. Tell yourself, "I deserve this. I'm worth it."

WRITING A LETTER

Write Yourself a Best Friend Letter. In connection with the prior concept of becoming your own best friend, write yourself a letter from this point of view. Select all of your best features. As the songwriter Johnny Mercer said a number of years ago, "Ya gotta accentuate the positive and eliminate the negative." Don't be afraid to praise yourself. After all, this letter is not intended for general circulation, but to give yourself a private boost.

Here is an example of one such letter, written by Melanie G.:

Dear Melanie:

I want to tell you how much I like you. You are one of the most kind-hearted people I know. You never forget to take care of others. You are loyal, steadfast, and true. You work hard at your career and are a competent professional person. You meet the emotional needs of your husband and your children. You are always there for them in dark moments. Also, you are a loyal friend.

Sometimes I know you don't think you're as attractive as other women. But it's not true. When you take a good, long look at yourself in the mirror you should see a person who has many good physical features. When you take the time out to dress correctly and use a little make up, you can still look pretty terrific. You have a pretty nose, large dark brown eyes, and a lovely smile.

And you're smart. Don't sell your intelligence short. It is definitely one of your prime attributes.

Love,
Your Best Friend,
Melanie

Melanie says, "Just writing the letter gave me a boost. I keep it in a secret place, and re-read it whenever I feel a little lonely."

Of course, your own best friend letter will have different details. But don't be afraid to pull out all of the stops in your own favor. Writing the letter is an automatic way to magnify your good points. Often we get into the bad mental habit of minimizing our good points and maximizing our negative ones. Writing the letter will help to restore a balance.

PEOPLE WHO ARE NURTURING

Concentrate Your Attention on People Who Are Nurturing. Why waste your time on people who have very little ability to nurture you? They can't help you overcome loneliness. Some people are warm, affectionate, and genuinely capable of expressing interest in others. They are the kinds of individuals you want to seek out. They have something to give. They are the people who will help you satisfy your stroke hunger. An emotional investment in such persons will not be wasted. It will be returned with, so to speak, interest.

BEING GENEROUS

Be Generous with Your Own Strokes. If you want positive strokes, be sure to give them. If you want a hug, give a hug. If you want a compliment, pay one. If you want praise, give praise. To a large extent, we receive in accordance with the way in which we give. If you are a loving person with your partner, there is a good chance you will be loved back. If you are attentive and interested when your friends talk, there is a good chance they will be attentive and interested when you talk.

But don't gush over people. When you praise, praise specifically. Avoid praising the other person's personality. Say, "I'm really enjoying this cake you baked." Don't say,

"You're such a wonderful cook. I wish I could cook as well as you do." Say, "I like the color of that dress." Don't say, "You're taste in clothes is incredible!" Say, "I got a kick out of the way you played that song on the guitar." Don't say, "You're such a fantastic musician." When you lay praise on like a thick, sticky jam, it is, like jam, gooey. The other person will feel uncomfortable. And instead of feeling stroked, he or she may very well feel patronized.

Do stroke other people. Do it correctly and intelligently, and you are likely to receive a generous share of strokes in return. And these will definitely help you conquer loneliness.

The Last Word

The poet Henry Wadsworth Longfellow wrote:

> *Talk not of wasted affection, affection never was wasted;*
>
> *If it enrich not the heart of another, its waters, returning*
>
> *Back to their springs, like the rain, shall fill them full of refreshment;*
>
> *That which the fountain sends forth returns again to the fountain.*

Longfellow's observations reinforce the last suggestion made in this chapter, "Be generous with your own strokes." Be a genuinely affectionate person. The gift of affection freely given to others is a value in its own right.

Key Points to Remember

▫— Institutionalized infants who do not receive enough affection often fail to thrive. This condition is called *hospitalism*.

▫— Like infants, you and I need affection in order to maintain a sense of well being.

▫— A *stroke* in transactional analysis is a unit of recognition.

▫— If you are in a state of *stroke hunger*, you will feel cut off from others, shut out of the ongoing stream of life.

▫— Think in terms of earning strokes.

▫— Don't try to get strokes from a stone-hearted person.

▫— Realize that sometimes it's OK to go outside of the home or a marriage to obtain strokes.

▫— Ask for strokes.

▫— Don't become addicted to negative strokes.

▫— If you have a tendency to be overweight, don't stroke yourself with food.

▫— Learn to stroke yourself.

▫— Write yourself a best friend letter.

▫— Concentrate on nurturing people.

▫— Be generous with your own strokes.

4 THE ART OF WINNING FRIENDS: HOW TO BE WELL LIKED

Eleven-year-old Lena comes home from school with a long, sad face. Her father asks, "What's wrong, Lena?"

Lena answers, "I don't have any friends."

"Really? I think—"

Lena interrupts. "Nobody likes me."

"Now I don't think that's true, dear."

"It is! It is!" And Lena heads for her room.

Seventeen-year-old Norris comes home from school with a long, sad face. His mother asks, "What's wrong, Norris?"

Norris answers, "I don't have any friends."

His mother says, "Oh, that can't be true. I would say—"

Norris interrupts. "Nobody likes me."

"No, no. Darling. People like you."

"You don't understand." And Norris leaves the room.

Thirty-four-year-old Judith, a single woman who lives alone, is riding the bus home from work. She sees her long, sad face reflected faintly in the window next to her seat. She is thinking, "I don't have any friends." And then she mentally adds, "Nobody seems to like me."

Lena, Norris, and Judith, ranging in age from eleven to thirty-four, are playing the same sad song. It is a song of self-pity characterized by the lament, "I don't have any friends. Nobody likes me."

Many people play some version of this song, aloud or silently. It is a song of suffering. And the more that one plays the song, the more one feels helpless and trapped by loneliness.

If you play some version of the "Nobody likes me" song, you don't have to keep playing it. There are explicit ways to become more well liked.

Interpersonal Attraction

Think about an inexpensive play magnet. It readily attracts small pieces of metal containing iron. Small pieces of wood, on the other hand, show no affinity for the magnet. Transfer the image of the magnet to human relations. We say of some people that they have a "magnetic" personality. They attract others to them.

On the other hand, there are some people who have no magnetism. They tend to be ignored by others. And, finally, there are people who are offensive. They are avoided by others.

What makes the difference among people who have personal magnetism and those who do not? Is it some mysterious something called "charisma?" Is it "allure," "charm," or "that certain something?" Are charisma and similar concepts beyond the range of psychological analysis? Or can they be reduced to behaviors that you can learn and acquire? Is there something you can *do* to be more attractive to others, to become well liked?

I am not going to argue that nebulous concepts such as those mentioned above can be reduced to a few behavioral elements. On the other hand, having said this, it should be noted that a behavioral analysis of interpersonal attraction *does* yield a rich payoff in the form of practical suggestions. Those suggestions will be presented in this chapter. And it is quite possible that if you want be more attractive to others, you will be able to do so. The way that people react to you is, to a large extent, *within your control*.

Winning Friends

Below you will find a list of interactive skills that will almost certainly increase your attractiveness to others. The term *attractiveness* is being used here in reference to your personality, not your physical appearance. Research suggests that one of the primary factors that draws one person to another is personality. Interestingly, research also suggests that if your personality is perceived as attractive, this has a positive effect on the other person's perception of your general appearance. Consequently, you are likely to find that the itemized skills will have a double benefit.

THE OTHER PERSON'S EGO

Remember That the Other Person Has an Ego. You are fully alive, conscious, and aware of the fact that you have an ego that doesn't relish being bruised, discounted, or otherwise abused. We frequently focus on this fact to the exclusion of the fact that the other person in your immediate social environment feels *exactly the same way.* Most people, to themselves, are the most important people in the world. You must remember this. One of the principal keys to increasing your interpersonal attractiveness is to concentrate your attention on the needs of the other individual's ego, not your own. Ask yourself, "What does he or she want? What would make this person feel important, valued, clever, or loved?" If you think you know, and more often than not the answer is obvious, then do it. Feed the other person's ego and you can almost see it expand.

Do not think of the above skill and those that are to follow as manipulative devices. On the contrary, they will help you attain your goal of winning friends only if they are applied with sincerity. You must be genuine. Most other people can spot a phony quite quickly. Think in terms of *caring* about other people.

If you realize that the other person has an ego that in its own way is as needy as your own, you are likely to become a more sensitive and compassionate person. The reason for this is that it is important for you to see the other person as *fully alive*, an actual living, breathing human being, not a sort of thing or object in your mental world.

CRITICISMS

Refrain From Making Obvious Criticisms. It is very easy to criticize, to find flaws. Often people who are openly critical think that this makes them perceived as intelligent in the other person's eyes. After all, only an intelligent person would be able to see so many things wrong in everything. Nothing could be farther from the truth. If you nitpick and find every little thing wrong with everything, you will be seen as petty and trivial in your approach to life. Big people let the little things go— *without comment*.

There is a certain tendency for critical persons to gain a bit of boldness when they achieve a little familiarity with another person. Often partners and friends are directly critical of the way in which another person walks, talks, dresses, and so forth. If the critic is challenged, or if irritation is expressed, then the critic becomes defensive. "I was only telling you for your own good." It is more likely that the criticism is a form of veiled hostility.

Ethan H. says, "I had a brief friendship once with a fellow named Harvey. It wasn't long before he was telling me that I shouldn't wear brown, that I had too many clothes with brown in them. Then he told me that I should cut my hair differently. In a restaurant, he tried to correct my table manners as if I was a child and he was the parent. Then he told me that a certain movie that I liked was stupid, that nobody of intelligence could possibly like this particular movie. I tell you that the guy so turned me off that I very quickly wanted nothing to do with him.

"Actually, he was hard to shake. I guess he liked having a scapegoat for his aggressions. He seemed genuinely hurt and bewildered by my lack of interest in him. And I didn't have the heart to tell him that his habit of being critical made him obnoxious. I suppose I should have. This probably would have been the decent thing to do. On the other hand, I'm sure this would have been offensive to him. He could dish out criticism, but I didn't have the impression that he'd be able to take much. So I just gave him a bunch of excuses for not getting together, and eventually he got the message and drifted away."

THE IMPORTANCE OF FEELING IMPORTANT

Make the Other Person Feel Important. Emily and Faith, coworkers, are having lunch together for the first time. They are both new on the job and would like to make some friends. Seated in a comfortable booth, the talk turns to family and children. Emily brings out a wallet thick with pictures and shows Faith photographs of her three children. Faith is completely bored, barely looks at the pictures, and makes no meaningful comments. Instead, restlessly, she fishes out her own wallet and soon is enthusiastically presenting pictures of her own children. Emily pretends to be interested in Faith's mini-album, but the truth is that she is offended. She feels very much discounted. She thinks that she must be very unimportant in Faith's eyes. And she's right, she is.

A few days later Emily is having lunch with another coworker, Glenda. Again, the subject of family and children comes up. This time Emily hesitates to display photographs of her children. Nonetheless, there is something about Glenda that gives her confidence. Soon she finds herself taking her wallet out of her purse. Glenda expresses an interest. "This is your oldest daughter? What lovely hair." A few minutes later she says, "This is your youngest son. And you say he's interested in music. How wonderful." Emily is glowing. And Glenda brings out no pictures of her own family. This first time all of the attention is given to Emily's family. Glenda wisely perceives that next time will be soon enough to talk about her own family.

Generally, other people will eventually give you "free information." They will try to talk about their partners, their children, their hobbies, what they read, where they have been, what movies they like, and so forth. If you pick up on any of these things, make a positive comment, and show an interest, then others will feel rewarded and encouraged. They will have been made to feel important, and you will have made yourself appealing to them.

The importance of feeling important can hardly be exaggerated. Most of us lead ordinary lives and do ordinary things. We go about our business on a daily basis without fanfare and red carpets. Yet we all know what the letters *VIP* stand for. If someone makes you feel that you are indeed a very important person in his or her eyes, you are likely to be attracted to that person.

One of the principal ways in which you can increase your interpersonal attractiveness to others is to create the impression that the other individual has significance and special worth to you. You do this by giving recognition to his or her expressed interests or values.

COMPLIMENTS

Pay Compliments Often. Be genuine about giving compliments. Don't make something up. Sincerely look for something in the other person that you actually admire, and then give it verbal expression. Here are just a few examples of the kinds of compliments that can be given, depending on the other person and the particular situation:

"I really enjoy driving with you. I can see you obey the rules of the road and don't take unnecessary risks. It makes me feel safe and secure."

"I get a kick out of the way in which you tell jokes. You don't waste a word and you get right to the point."

"I enjoy listening to you talk about world affairs. You are so much more informed that the average person. And you are able to organize your ideas in a way that cuts right through all of the political nonsense to the heart of the matter."

"Thanks for letting me read your poem. It really touched my heart. I wish I could express myself in this way. It's a real talent, one that you should cherish."

"Your apple pie was delicious, the best I've had in a long time. Thanks for having me over for dinner. It was a real treat."

"You're lawn is so green and thick and free of weeds! I'm going to have to ask you to teach me what the trick is."

"Your son Bill is a very warm and polite young man. It just does my heart good to talk to him for even a few minutes."

If a natural compliment comes to your lips, don't hold it back. Let the other person know how you feel.

Don't confuse giving a compliment with flattery. The *Funk and Wagnall's Standard College Dictionary* defines the word *compliment* as follows: "An expression of admiration, praise, or congratulation." The word *flattery* is defined as follows: "The act of flattering; excessive, often insincere praise or expression of admiration." As you can see from the definitions, a compliment is genuine and flattery is not.

Often we hold back a compliment, fearing that it will be misinterpreted as flattery. However, if the compliment is an honest one, and if we keep it to specific facts, it will almost certainly be received in the spirit in which it was given.

TALKING ABOUT YOURSELF

Avoid Talking About Yourself. Focus your attention and interest on the other person, not yourself. Although you are certainly fascinated with your vacation, your trip, your children, your partner, what movie you saw over the weekend, where you ate dinner last night, and so forth, the other person is not. It is sometimes difficult to believe that other people will be completely bored by what interests you so much. Oh, if they are polite, they will *pretend* to be interested. But usually they have to work at it if you go on too long.

Why are people so bored, for example, by a description of the vacation time you spent in a fascinating city? The answer is that they are receiving the information *second hand*. The other individual cannot see what you saw, taste the foods you ate, and so forth. Therefore what sparkles for you falls flat from a second-hand viewpoint.

To expand on the above idea, let's say that you start to describe at length a very funny movie you saw. As you talk about it you can't help laughing. Have you ever noticed that the other person is *not* laughing? Or, if he or she is, it is somewhat polite, forced laughter. Again, the reason is that the listener is receiving only a faint carbon copy of your experience.

Talking about your experiences and highly specific personal interests is perceived by others as a form of egotism. It seems to them that you think you're *so* important. And they find your preoccupation with self offensive.

Frederick O., a fifty-eight-year-old astronomy professor, says, "I learned the hard way how talking too much about an interest can turn another person off. I was

reading science fiction long before science fiction was popular. When I was an adolescent I used to read *Thrilling Wonder Stories* and *Astounding Science Fiction*, and I thought the ideas in the stories were wonderful. I didn't have many friends in high school. I used to talk incessantly about science fiction to anybody who would listen. One young woman who condescended to date me finally told me about halfway through the date, 'Must you keep talking about all those stupid rocket ships and time machines? It's so *boring*.' She hit me right between the eyes. And I haven't forgotten the lesson I learned. Today I can talk about space and the stars to my heart's content, because I teach the subject. But I only go on and on to *a classroom of students*. I remember that my friends and family aren't my students. And I pay attention more to what they are interested in than what I am interested in."

Does all of this mean that you should never talk about yourself and your interests? Of course not. In fact, to go this far would make you be perceived as unnatural and lacking in authenticity. Allow the persons to talk about themselves and their interests *first*. Subsequently, you can talk a little about yourself and your interests. But do it *sparingly*. A little goes a long way.

SMILING

Smile Frequently. Rate the power of a smile highly when you are trying to win a friend. A genuine smile communicates silently a world of meaning. It can say, depending on the situation, "I'm interested in you," "I'm paying attention," "I like you," "I'm amused," or "I'm really enjoying myself." A smile is a ray of emotional sunshine, and the other person will bask in it.

A familiar proverb says, "Laugh and the world laughs with you. Cry and you cry alone." The same can be said of smiling. If you frown, you add a stone to the side of a scale that tips in the direction of loneliness. A smile, on the other hand, helps you to overcome isolation.

We tend to think of smiles as natural expressions of our feelings. Consequently, the advice to smile consciously might seem forced. However, it can be argued that some people are not in the habit of smiling. If they will make a conscious decision to smile, when appropriate, they may find that smiles eventually *do* become natural and subconsciously controlled. A well-known theory of emotions, the James-Lange theory, says that it makes as much sense to say that actions determine feelings as to say that feelings determine actions. Consequently, if you will yourself to smile, you may very well find that your emotional state tends to follow along and catch up with your action.

Perhaps this is why the comedian Charlie Chaplin wrote in his song "Smile" the following: "Smile though your heart is breaking." He had endured many hardships in his life, and he had learned that smiling, maintaining an optimistic outer posture, helped him to keep going and to see things through.

The author Wilbur D. Nesbit wrote:

> *The thing that goes the farthest toward making life worth while,*
>
> *That costs the least, and does the most, is just a pleasant smile.*

Make it a point to smile more often when you are with another person whom you like, and watch this behavior help to convert an acquaintance into a friend.

EYE CONTACT

Make Good Eye Contact When You Are Conversing. Eye contact is one of the primary ways in which you communicate to others that you are interested in them and what they have to say. Eye contact need not be unflinchingly steady. In fact if you gaze into another person's eyes without a break, eventually the other person will feel uncomfortable. He or she will usually involuntarily break eye contact.

Studies of eye contact behavior suggest that the following is a comfortable pattern. Look directly into another person's eyes for about fifteen or twenty seconds. Follow this with a three- to five-second break. Then resume eye contact for fifteen or twenty seconds. Then break again. And continue in this manner. Of course, most of this is habitual. But if you are a person who tends to look away too long and too often when others talk to you, then you might reexamine your eye contact behavior. If you make poor eye contact when another person is speaking, this will be interpreted as lack of interest on your part. It will often be perceived as mildly insulting.

On the other hand, if you maintain good eye contact, it is a way of saying "Continue. I'm interested." Eye contact provides the other person with constant feedback that sustains and encourages that person's expression of self. When you give another person good eye contact you are providing that individual with a high-quality psychological reward.

Let's say that you are eating out with someone else. If you sit side by side in the same booth it is very difficult to maintain good eye contact. So avoid this kind of seating. If you sit directly across from the other person, this is better. Eye contact can be maintained easily and broken relatively easily. Interestingly, research suggests that the best seating position, when there are only two people eating together, is at a forty-five-degree angle to each other. This makes it easy to turn the head slightly toward the other person when making eye contact. And it is equally easy to turn the head slightly away from the other person when breaking eye contact. The seating is natural, and you should try to arrange it whenever practical. (Note that this kind of seating requires either a table or a horseshoe-shaped booth.)

ACTIVE LISTENING

Acquire the Art of Active Listening. Active listening is a skill that includes what was described above, making good eye contact. When you make good eye contact, you communicate to the other person that you *are* listening. Along with good eye contact, active listening involves other specific behaviors. These are indicated below.

Nod Your Head Often. Head nodding is one of the ways in which you communicate that you are following the other person's line of thought. It provides a constant source of (believe it or not) high-quality feedback that lets the other person know you are making sense out of what he or she is saying. It also is a kind of subtle encouragement.

Say "Uh-huh" Frequently. Like head nodding, uh-huhs also provide feedback and encouragement. Each uh-huh provides a bit of support and keeps others motivated to talk. Their use is particularly important on the telephone when the other person cannot get cues from eye contact and facial expression.

So important are uh-huhs that they have been used to produce an experimental effect called the *Greenspoon effect.* The Greenspoon effect takes place when one person's verbal behavior is intentionally shaped by another person. For example, in one experiment, two people were taped as they had a conversation. The first person was instructed to say "Uh-huh" every time the second person uttered a plural noun. Recordings revealed quite clearly that, motivated by the first person's encouragement, the second person began to utter plural nouns significantly more frequently. And the first person did this quite sub-consciously, without distinct awareness.

Say "Mm-mmm" From Time to Time. The murmur "Mm-mmm" is a kind of fuzzy feedback. It has borderline audibility, but is usually picked up. Other persons tend to perceive it as a form of comprehension on your part. They also tend to think that you are seriously mulling over what they are saying. And they feel that they are being taken seriously.

State the Emotional Content of the Other Person's Message. Let's say that Nelson is telling a story about how his father did something to him that was quite unfair and arbitrary. At the end of the story, assuming the comment fits, say, "I hear a lot of anger in your voice." If you are satisfied that this is obviously correct, this will be perceived by Nelson as a very satisfying comment.

In general, the big three emotional states tend to be anger, anxiety, and worry. If you decode the verbal content of other people's remarks, you can offer a comment that reveals you understand their emotional state.

Match the Other Person's Facial Expression. When you are listening to someone else talk, make a conscious effort to match, within reasonable limits, the other individual's facial expression. If the other person is smiling, smile. If the other person is telling a long, sad story with a frown, then frown from time to time. No, others won't think you are making fun of them. On the contrary, you will be perceived as being a person with that rare quality called *empathy*, the ability to tune in to another person's emotional wavelength.

BEING AUTHENTIC

Be Rewarding to Others, But Not Excessively So. The preceding recommendations were based to a large extent on a theory of interpersonal attraction that the social psychologist Elliot Aronson called the *reward-cost theory*. The reward-cost theory says that a first person will be well liked by a second person if the first person is rewarding to the second person with very little cost to the second person. And, on the whole, the reward-cost theory makes sense. It is practical and useful, and can be readily applied to improve human relations.

However, a correction is needed. If you are excessively rewarding to another person with little or no cost to that individual, you are likely to eventually be taken for granted. You may even end up getting used and abused. So you want to introduce a note of authenticity. As I have already said, be genuine. Don't give compliments or smiles or other psychological rewards if you don't think they are merited by the other person.

As a counterbalance to the reward-cost theory, it is possible to include in our thinking what Aronson called the *gain-loss theory*. Aronson writes, "My idea is a very simple one. It suggests that increases in positive, rewarding behavior from another person have more impact on an individual than constant, invariant reward from that person." In other words, it is OK to be real, to be authentic. You will be taken more seriously. And when you provide the other individual with rewarding behavior, it will be appreciated. Make an effort to find the happy medium between being excessively rewarding and not rewarding enough.

The Last Word

If you can't seem to form friendships, don't be discouraged. There is a lot you can do to improve the state of your personal life. You don't have to accept conditions as they are. Much is within your own control.

The art of winning friends is just that, an *art*. And that art consists of a set of learnable social skills. The principal skills were identified and described in this chapter. If you make a conscious effort to apply these skills, you will find yourself getting better and better at using them. And you will find that it is not at all difficult to win friends.

Key Points to Remember

□┉ This chapter lists a set of interactive skills that will increase your attractiveness to others.

□┉ Remember that the other person has an ego.

□┉ Refrain from making obvious criticisms.

□┉ Make the other person feel important.

□┉ Pay compliments often.

□┉ Avoid talking about yourself.

□┉ Smile frequently.

□┉ Make good eye contact when you are conversing.

□┉ Acquire the art of active listening. Nod your head often. Say "Uh-huh" and "Mm-mmm" frequently. State the emotional content of the other person's message. Match the other person's facial expression.

□┉ Be rewarding to others, but not excessively so.

5 THE OUTSIDER: OVERCOMING ALIENATION

Do you often feel that you are an outsider?

Do you sometimes look at people you supposedly know well and have the disconcerting impression that you don't know them at all, that they are strangers? Do you from time to time feel *apart* from others?

If so, you are experiencing some degree of alienation. *Alienation* is, as suggested by the above questions, a feeling of apartness, of estrangement from others. The word *lien* refers to something that ties one thing to another. In law, for example, a lien ties an instrument such as a mortgage to a piece of property. Consequently, when a person is alienated, that person is without ties. The alienated person is like a castaway—emotionally disconnected from either the family or other reference groups.

It is distressing to be alienated. And alienation is an important factor in loneliness. It is next to impossible to be alienated and simultaneously free from the burden of loneliness. Alienation and loneliness go together like two sides of the same coin.

The problem of alienation is presented in a harsh and compelling way in the existential philosopher Jean-Paul Sartre's novel *Nausea*. In the opening pages of the book we meet the historian Antoine Roquentin. Roquentin is disgusted with existence. There seems to be no reason for either things or people to exist. This rejection of everything is a kind of emotional nausea. Roquentin is a reflection of Sartre's own life as a young man. Sartre did not bow down to alienation. He fought back and eventually connected with life and others.

Understanding Alienation

Alienation is a plague of modern times. It has been a subject of substantial concern to psychologists, philosophers, sociologists, and novelists. A number of factors contribute to it. Below you will find three examples of such factors. This listing is not complete, but is provided to convey the idea that, within limits, alienation *is* an explainable phenomenon.

A first factor that contributes to alienation is transplant shock. Imagine a plant thriving in its familiar place. Now transplant it and there may be problems. Maybe it begins to shrivel and become sickly. Something like this happens when the nuclear family moves away from a familiar territory to an unfamiliar one. A husband, wife, and children detached from a larger family consisting of grandparents, aunts and uncles, cousins, and so forth has to nurture itself. Often the individuals in the family become alienated not only from the larger family but from each other. Sociologists have taken particular note of this phenomenon.

A second factor that contributes to alienation is the conviction that one is superior in some way to one's associates. If you get to thinking that you are a lot smarter than your partner, your coworkers, or your friends, you will begin to distance yourself from them. You don't respect them or their opinions.

A third factor that can contribute to alienation is to have a depersonalizing job. If the work you do does not satisfy your creative needs, does not require you to use your intelligence adequately, you can feel something like a robot. Routine work that presents no challenge can be deadening. As you go numb inside, you feel a kind of general numbness toward others. Feeling a little less than human, it is difficult to relate to others in a human way.

As already indicated, these factors are by no means all of the important ones that could be identified. However, our goal is to focus on *how* alienation can be overcome.

As this important process is discussed, additional causal factors in alienation will naturally emerge.

Overcoming Alienation

A state of alienation is often linked to feelings of powerlessness and helplessness. An alienated person has an impression of being cut off, adrift. The lyricist Lorenz Hart once wrote a song with the title, "A Ship Without a Sail." The singer of the song says that he or she is all at sea, lost, and unable to go anywhere but in circles. To some extent, the lyric reflected problems experienced by Hart himself.

But you don't have to be a ship without a sail. You can take a stand against the kinds of factors that contribute to alienation.

THE POWER OF BELIEVING

Reject the Idea That You Are Powerless and Helpless. If you approach alienation from a "poor me" attitude, you can't overcome it. Self-pity will only make the problem worse. It is important to realize that, from the psychological point of view, you are never completely powerless. And you are never completely helpless. You need to assert that you have a free will, that you are an autonomous human being capable of making real choices. You need to *believe* that you have the ability to neutralize those emotional factors that contribute to alienation. This is a very important first step.

The power of believing is enormous. If you genuinely believe that you can overcome alienation, the odds are quite high that you will actually be able to do so. And the belief that you can overcome alienation is *not* an illusion. It *can* be done. I already mentioned that the philosopher Sartre was successful. And his alienation was profound.

LOOKING FOR THE BEST

Look for the Best in Other Members of a Group. We are social creatures. The psychologist Alfred Adler said that social interest is an inborn aspect of human behavior. We have a deep need to make contact at both a cognitive and an emotional level with others. This need tends to be satisfied by group identification. We see ourselves as belonging to a family, a club, an organization, and so forth. This sense of belonging is undermined when we become critical of certain features of the group.

The criticism usually emerges in the form of dissatisfaction with certain individuals. We think, "Harry wants to run the whole show," or "My husband is too critical," or "My children are a bunch of brats," or "The foreman thinks he's a little dictator," or "The captain has no real regard for the crew."

In connection with the last quotation, in Herman Wouk's novel *The Caine Mutiny* the crew is in rebellion against Captain Queeq, a petty tyrant. One of the important points that is brought out at the court martial of Lieutenant Myrak, the executive officer who repudiated Queeg's authority, is that the crew focused only on what Queeg did wrong. They exaggerated his faults and minimized his good points. In fact they aggravated their alienation from Queeg and this led to the eventual rupture and disaster that took the form of a mutiny.

We tend to magnify faults and minimize good points. Make an effort to reverse this process. Look for the best features in members of a group and it will undercut the process leading toward alienation.

SOCIAL GROUPS

Seek to Identify with Social Groups That Reflect the Values of the Larger Culture. A social group—for example, a club, an organization, or a church congregation—functions much like a family. If you identify with the group, its interests and its values become your own. If you identify with a group that is traditional, you will have no problems. Not only will you acquire the sense of belongingness that is antagonistic to alienation, you will also be at peace with the general society.

But what if you identify with a gang, an organization, a cult, or a secret society that is at odds with the larger culture? You *will* overcome alienation to some extent. Members of the splinter group will become false kin; they will feel like brothers and sisters. But it is likely that you will be alienated on a bigger life canvas. You are likely to be on the outs with parents, other relatives, and old friends. And when the deviant group runs into a harsh clash with the larger culture, as it often does, your fortunes will be tied to it. If there is suffering involved, you will be forced to share in it. If your only lifeboat is sinking, you will go down with it.

So pick a group carefully. For your own protection, make sure that it fits into the general society in some meaningful way.

TRADITION

If You Have Fallen Away From Them, Reconsider Traditional Values. Think back to Tevye in *Fiddler on the Roof.* He sings with passion and conviction of the importance of tradition. One of the ways in which we overcome alienation is by heart-felt acceptance of traditional values.

What are traditional values? In an individual case, a person doesn't have to search very far. You were probably taught a set of values by your family. And most families reflect the principal values of the larger culture. In the main, these are obvious: Be a responsible parent, accept the teachings of your religion, have respect for your partner, and so forth. Traditional values are so obvious that they are almost invisible, and, as a consequence, it is easy to lose sight of them.

Paula F. says, "I went through a very lonely, rough time a few years ago. I felt trapped in a loveless marriage, and I wanted *out*. I had married when I was seventeen, had three children, and was a full-time homemaker. When I divorced, I thought I had had it with kids. I wanted nothing to do with them. I know it sounds awful, but I didn't care about either my husband or my children.

"I remember saying to him, 'Now it's my turn. I've helped you get established in your career. Now I'm going to school without the excess baggage of you or the kids.' He was only too willing to take on the full custody I offered him. He considered me an unfit mother—and, in a way, I guess I was.

"I went to school, worked part time, and became an accountant. I dated a string of guys—mostly losers I must admit. And then the chickens came home to roost. After a few years, I couldn't stand being alienated from my children. I was sinking. A strange ennui gripped me and nothing seemed worth doing. Life was lonely and joyless.

"I took a long, hard look at myself and realized that I had dumped an important traditional value in a cavalier fashion: a mother's responsibility toward her children.

"I knew I had to reconnect with my children. And little by little I have. I approached them and my ex-husband on the basis of 'How can I help you? What can I do for you?' At first they didn't trust me. Trust, when broken, is awfully hard to rebuild.

"I was smart enough to avoid a lot of self-pitying remarks like, 'I've missed you so much,' or 'I need you.' I've also avoided self-blaming remarks such as, 'I know I've been an awful mother.' I decided that if I just came forth, really became a resource for them, I would overcome my alienation from them.

"And I have. I'm a responsible mother now. I was a very lonely, bitter woman for just a little too long. But things·are much better now."

The concept of *return* is very important. If you have strayed away from them, return to the values that are rooted in your particular background, and alienation will be short-circuited.

RECONCILIATION

If You Are on the Outs With Someone You Once Loved, Take Steps to Effect a Reconciliation. Perhaps, like Paula, you are on the outs with a person or persons you once loved or cared about. You may have a parent, a brother, a sister, an old friend, or someone else that you haven't talked to in months or years. Maybe an old grudge has been keeping you apart. If the rip in the fabric of your relationship is experienced as a kind of nagging unpleasantness in your existence, it may be time to work on patching things up. Even if you have been alienated for quite a while, it is quite possible that it's not too late to reconnect.

Perhaps you are thinking, "The other person is so cold and hostile. Why didn't he or she take the first step?" This is a fair question. But why didn't *you* take the first step? Is it because *you* are cold and hostile? Or is it because you are afraid that you will be rebuffed? Chances are that's it. Be sure you realize that the other person is in the same psychological position that you are in.

It's a no-win situation, a double bind. Each of you is afraid to take the first step. Both of you would like to reconcile. But neither of you makes a move. Your alienation from each other is frozen in time.

Someone has to take the first step in order to break the barrier between you. It might as well be you. True, you might be rebuffed. Prepare yourself for this possibility. And tell yourself you can handle it if you have to. On the other hand, if you don't *do* something, the canyon between you may remain there until the day you die. Before you refuse to act, ask yourself if you are willing to go to your death in a state of alienation from someone who, at some level of your being, you really love.

A warm, friendly letter is a good way to start. Jonathan H. says, "I hadn't talked to my brother Thomas for over five years. We had feuded over cutting up the family farm after Mom and Dad died. I accused him of being stupid. And he accused me of being greedy."

Here is the letter that Jonathan wrote to his brother:

Dear Thomas:

> *Hello. How are you? I hope you and the family are well. We're all OK.*

> *Thomas, I've been thinking about you a lot lately. And I want you to know I miss you. We are brothers and I know we love each other. I think back often to the happy days when we were both kids growing up on the farm. We had each other then. We were more than brothers. We were pals.*

> *I don't know about you, but I miss my pal. Read this letter. Think about it a little bit. And let's just forget our past misunderstandings. I won't bring them up if you don't.*

> *I'll call you in about a week. And we'll see if we can get together.*

> *Love,*

> *Jonathan*

Jonathan didn't have to wait a week. He got a phone call from Thomas only three days after Jonathan mailed the letter. Thomas felt exactly the way Jonathan did, and Thomas expressed pleasure at receiving the letter. A meeting time and place were arranged, and they were on their way to a reconciliation.

PHYSICAL DISTANCE

Don't Allow the Barrier of Physical Distance to Contribute to a Progressive Alienation From the People You Really Care About. Friends and relatives often live

many miles apart. There is a certain tendency to allow the sheer physical distance to be a roadblock to communication. But in this day and age of electronics it need not be this way. To the extent that your finances allow it, make the cost of regular telephone calls or the use of electronic mail a part of your budget. This is more than a luxury. Maintaining close ties with the significant people in your life is an important part of living.

You may not have a computer with a modem, and, consequently, can't use electronic mail. I recommend you explore the costs and possibilities of this kind of mail. Its virtue is that it is almost instantaneous. It is very reinforcing to be in a mode that allows for rapid exchanges of ideas. It is very much like talking on the phone. Some people actually prefer it at times to telephone conversations.

And, of course, don't neglect conventional resources such as the old-fashioned method of writing and mailing letters. Photographs, audiotapes, and videotapes can also be sent by mail. I know all of this requires a bit of effort. And it is easy to procrastinate. However, assuming individuals on the receiving end reciprocate at least some of the time, the emotional payoff you receive more than compensates for the effort you make.

Don't let physical distance allow you to lose a relationship with a parent, a child, a brother or sister, or a close friend.

SUPERIORITY

Get Rid of a Secret Sense of Superiority. Alienated persons often possess a secret sense of superiority. They think that they are smarter than other members of a social reference group, and draw back from closeness as a result. They distance themselves from the family, their coworkers, or members of a club in order to feel *above* them. By placing themselves psychologically outside of the group they feel free to heap secret scorn on the group, silently laughing at them and their foibles.

Examine your attitudes, and attempt to discern whether or not you discover a secret sense of superiority among them. Do you think you are smarter or more clever than other people? Do you often think, "Oh what fools ye mortals be?" Do you quickly find fault in the things that other people do? Do you have a lot of criticisms of the behavior of other people?

To some extent a secret sense of superiority is enjoyable. It makes you feel better than other people. However, there is also a price to pay. And that price is alienation. You can't stand psychologically apart from a group and at the same time *identify* with that group. And if you don't identify, you will, to a large extent, be alienated. You may go through all of the motions, but they will be superficial, and the distressing sense of being an outsider will nag at you.

Recognize that you are *not* superior to other people. Yes, you may have domains of behavior in which you are more effective or more skilled than they are. But they will almost certainly have domains of behavior in which they are more effective or more skilled than you are. Try to get away from the idea of superiority. Instead of thinking in terms of inferiority and superiority, think in terms of value-free individual differences. This will help you be less judgmental, and will bring you closer to others. It will help you overcome alienation and will undercut loneliness.

A DEPERSONALIZING ENVIRONMENT

Seek Eventual Escape From a Depersonalizing Environment. A depersonalizing environment is one that makes you feel less like a human being and more like a thing or a robot. This can be a principal factor in alienation. A depersonalizing environment is not an objective fact, but a perception about the world. An environment that is pleasing to one person will be depersonalizing to

another. For example, some individuals seek and enjoy a military career. They thrive on it. They find themselves expanding and becoming more of a person. Others find it depersonalizing. To illustrate, James Jones, author of *From Here to Eternity*, found that a military environment went against his personal and emotional grain. His novel portrays the army as creating a depersonalizing environment, one that robs a member of his or her individuality. James Jones did not reenlist in the army, and pursued a career as a creative writer.

If you are in a depersonalizing environment, you will sometimes experience the feeling that you have been *reduced* in some way. Glen I. says, "I once worked as a social worker for the bureau of public assistance in a large city. I took the job as a stop gap. I was having a difficult time defining my vocational goals. I was hired because you had to have a bachelor's degree at the time in order to be a social worker, and I qualified. However, I had not had prior training as a social worker, nor did I have an interest in pursuing this career.

"After a two-week short course, I was put on the job. I was responsible for almost two hundred general relief cases. Later, I worked with unwed mothers. The sheer press of humanity was overwhelming. And there were more than fifty social workers on the premises. After a few months I remember thinking, 'I feel like a little worker ant. I'm just a programmed machine, one of thousands all over the country doing a similar job. I don't find this work creative or challenging. This job makes me feel like *nothing.'*

"It is not to my credit, but I had a similarly jaundiced view of my clients. I was unable to rise to the occasion. One of my coworkers, a woman named Johanna, had been a social worker for eight years and thrived on it. She felt she was doing meaningful, important work.

"When I eventually left the job to pursue other opportunities, I felt relieved and grateful. And I was glad that this world had a few Johannas to carry on work that made me feel useless and trivial."

Apparently Johanna thrived on being a social worker. Glen did not. He did the wise thing by escaping what was for him a depersonalizing environment.

If, based upon the above considerations, you experience a given social environment as depersonalizing, you will almost certainly be in a state of alienation. And, like James Jones or Glen, you want to seek eventual escape from it.

The Last Word

Alienation is always alienation *from.* The troubled individual is alienated from a partner, a child, a parent, a

sibling, a friend, a group, or even the general culture. A person who suffers from profound alienation feels like an outsider. One has the impression that he or she is an emotional foreigner even in physically familiar surroundings. One man who suffered from alienation described it this way: "It's as if I'm walking down a strange new street in a neighborhood that I both know and don't know. I look in windows and see smiling faces and warm rooms. They seem to be people I once knew. But nowhere am I welcome. I can look in, but I can't get in."

If you suffer from alienation, it doesn't have to be endured. You can overcome alienation by using the self-directed strategies presented in this chapter. They are practical, and they will be effective.

Key Points to Remember

◻—— Alienation is a feeling of apartness, of estrangement from others.

◻—— It is next to impossible to be alienated and simultaneously free from the burden of loneliness.

◻—— Examples of factors that contribute to alienation include (1) transplant shock, (2) the conviction that one is superior in some way to one's associates, and (3) a depersonalizing job.

◻—— Reject the idea that you are powerless and helpless.

◻—— Look for the best in other members of a group.

◻—— Seek to identify with social groups that reflect the values of the larger culture.

◻—— If you have fallen away from them, reconsider traditional values.

◻—— If you are on the outs with someone you once loved, take steps to effect a reconciliation.

⊐⊷ Don't allow the barrier of physical distance to contribute to a progressive alienation from the people you really care about.

⊐⊷ Get rid of a secret sense of superiority.

⊐⊷ Seek eventual escape from a depersonalizing environment.

6 POPULARITY IS NOT THE ANSWER: BECOMING AN INDIVIDUAL

The singer Mel Torme's book *Over the Rainbow* is a memoir of his friendship with Judy Garland. If there was ever anyone who enjoyed great popularity, it was Garland. She was the star of one of America's favorite movies, *The Wizard of Oz*. At the height of her career she was able to fill large auditoriums such as the London Palladium with a throng of admirers. More than once she sat on the edge of the stage, talking *with* and singing *to* her audience. They had a strong impression of intimacy and emotional closeness with this great star.

And yet she would call Torme in the small hours of the morning, seeking a little human warmth. He would drive over and visit with her, helping her overcome her nearly unbearable loneliness.

It is common for lonely persons to think that a possible antidote to their negative state is to achieve a state of greater popularity. Indeed, those who suffer from loneliness often *crave* popularity in somewhat the same way that an isolated traveler on the desert, one who has drunk the canteen dry, craves water. The fantasy is that the recognition and admiration and applause of many people will make one feel secure, accepted—even loved.

That fantasy is bankrupt.

The poem *Richard Cory* by Edwin Arlington Robinson tells of a wealthy, handsome man in a small town who is popular and admired by all. The narrator says that the people in the town were poor and miserable, that they envied Richard Cory. They worked and felt sorry for themselves because they couldn't afford meat, only bread. The poem concludes by saying that Richard Cory, on a calm summer night, went home and put a bullet through his head.

Was Richard Cory lonely? The poem is not explicit on this point. It deliberately leaves to our imagination *why* Richard Cory killed himself. It would seem, however, reading between the lines of the poem, that indeed he *was* lonely. In any event, his popularity did not save him from whatever emotional state drove him to suicide.

One of my counseling clients, Georgia F., told me, "I was one of the most popular students in my high school. Nothing would do but that I *must* be a cheerleader *and* have an important part in the senior musical. My boyfriend was the captain of the football team. It seemed I knew everybody on campus. I had a smile and a hello for everyone.

"I say I knew everybody. But this is wrong. I didn't *know* anybody. They were all acquaintances. And they certainly didn't know me. Even the relationship with my boyfriend was a farce. I didn't really have anything in common with him. I think I went with him because he was a trophy. He was a "catch," and I knew that a lot of the other girls envied me. We broke up shortly after we graduated. And it didn't hurt him much, I'm sure. I think he went with me because I was a kind of trophy too.

"I was very popular in high school. And I was also very, very lonely. A contradiction? Not at all. If and when I have children, I'm going to tell them to forget about popularity. It's no big deal. Believe me. I know, I've been there."

Coping Strategies

If you crave popularity, thinking that it will help you conquer loneliness, the coping strategies presented below will help you get over the craving.

Or, if you already *are* popular, and wonder why you still feel lonely, the suggestions will help you understand why a seeking-to-be-popular approach isn't working. Also, the coping strategies will help you get over an addiction to popularity, an artificial need for the approval of a lot of people.

DEFINING POPULARITY

Develop a Deeper Understanding of the Word Popular. The word *popular* is first cousin to the word *population.* A formal definition of a population in statistical work is "Any well-defined group." In order to be popular, one must be "known" or recognized by all or most of the members of a well-defined group. The group need not reach into the hundreds. For example, in beauty pageants it is common to vote one of fifty contestants, for example, "Miss Popularity." It is also possible to speak of the most popular person in a club, a small town, a college, a place of employment, and so forth.

The larger the group, the more bases you must touch in order to be popular.

Consequently, in order to be popular among a fairly large group of people, you have to spread yourself thin. This is one of the reasons why politicians and movie stars often feel lonely. As one movie star said, "I sometimes feel that everybody wants a piece of me and there isn't enough to go around. I feel like I'm one pat of butter, and I've got to get smeared on thousands of pieces of bread."

This is one of the difficulties with popularity. The larger the group, the more you are required to have superficial contacts with a lot of people. These contacts are not meaningful in themselves; their only purpose is to feed the craving for popularity. Although there are exceptions, there is a certain tendency for popularity to water down *all* relationships, including ones that should be particularly deep and meaningful.

So, understanding that the word *popular* automatically has built into it a facile surface quality, some of its attraction and value to you should be undermined.

≈≈≈ ≈≈≈ ≈≈≈ ≈≈≈ ≈≈≈ ≈≈≈ ≈≈≈ ≈≈≈ ≈≈≈

PLEASING OTHERS

Remember That You Can't Please Everyone. A major difficulty with popularity is that you have to try to please too many people. Abraham Lincoln made some penetrating observations about the difficulty of fooling people for very long. Borrowing his logic and applying it to pleasing, not fooling, people, we arrive at this proposition: "It is possible to please some of the people all of the time. And it is possible to please all of the people some of the time. But it is impossible to please all of the people all of the time."

If you try to please all of the people in a group, you will make yourself miserable. Some people try to do it. And it simply can't be done.

BEING LIKED

Reject the Idea That You Need to Be Liked by Everyone. Albert Ellis, principal founder of rational-emotive behavior therapy, says that a cardinal irrational idea is this one: It is a dire necessity for an adult human to be loved or approved of by virtually every significant other person in his or her life. The craving for popularity is even more irrational. Here the craving for approval extends beyond significant people to *every* human contact.

Chester L. is the owner of a hardware store in a small town. His father owned the store before him. Chester says, "I've always been a pleaser. When I was a child, my mother used to say to her sisters, 'The thing I like about Chester is that he's so *nice.*' A few years ago I was elected mayor. It was the culmination of years of cultivating people and belonging to organizations. I was the *mayor*, in my mind the most popular person in town.

"I kept trying to please everybody, to be nice to everybody. I don't think I fully realized that sometimes a mayor, as head of the city council, has to make some hard decisions. An effective mayor just can't please everybody.

"After about seven months in office I developed a serious case of high blood pressure. My doctor told me that I was at increased risk of a heart attack or a stroke. He explained that there was no organic basis for my condition, that it was probably stress induced.

"And the worst part of it all was that everything I was doing was making me feel lonely, not loved and accepted. I couldn't keep everybody happy. Even my wife pulled back to some extent. I remember one day she said, 'Chester, you've become a vain, superficial individual.' I began feeling very sorry for myself and somehow separated from everybody.

"I decided that I had one of two choices. I could resign as mayor, but to me this would be defeat. Or I could be an effective mayor, not a crowd pleaser. If I didn't get reelected for a second term, so be it. Well, I began to work at being a real mayor. And most of my tension and loneliness went away.

"Incidentally, I *did not* get reelected. I'm happy just running the hardware store. My blood pressure's normal again. I've got my loyal boosters and those who don't like me much. But that's OK. Business is about the same as it's always been."

It *is* important to be liked. But you don't have to be liked by *everybody*.

ENVY

Don't Envy Popular People Their Social Stardom. Popular people stand out. They are noticed and visible. Studies by the psychiatrist J. P. Moreno resulted in the development of a methodology called *sociograms*. A sociogram is a map of the social relationships in a group. For example, in a grammar school class the children are asked to write down the three names of other children they would most like to sit next to. Let's say that there are thirty children in the class. The researcher sorts through the responses and finds the name of a child who was picked most often. That child's name is placed in the center of a large piece of paper, and a circle is drawn around the name. The names of children who picked the most popular child are placed near that child, and each name is also circled. An arrow is drawn from each child to the three he or she picked.

The resulting graphic pattern, or sociogram, can be very revealing. If a particular child is picked by many other children, that child is called a *star*. There may be one or two or even three stars in a classroom, but seldom more. Often a given child will pick the star, but not be picked by the star. In fact this circumstance *must* arise in the case of stars because the star only picks three, in accordance with instructions, but may be picked by fifteen.

Children who are not picked by any other children are called *isolates*. It is rather obvious that isolates are usually lonely. However, it is somewhat less obvious to note that stars are also frequently lonely. Stardom removes them from being just regular kids to being something special. They have a burden to carry. People want something from them, and often they find it difficult to deliver. It is stressful to be the center of attention, to be expected to participate in activities instigated by others. There isn't enough "down time" just to be yourself. Also, stars can get addicted to the admiration and attention of others, and they may not adequately develop their own inner resources.

What has been said about star children is true in general. Stardom at any age or in any arena of life is a burden. It is not something to be wished for. People who have it often see it as much as a curse as a blessing.

T. S. Eliot, author of *The Waste Land*, is thought to have been one of the greatest poets of the twentieth century. In a biographical sketch, the author Norman Donaldson says, "He was a strange, private and often bewildered man who was raised into a cultural guru." The role of guru and its accompanying fame sat neither well nor lightly on Eliot's shoulders. All evidence suggests that it aggravated a persistent sense of emotional isolation.

Think for a moment about an actual star, one that you can see in the sky. Stars are in fact blazing suns. The nearest sun to us is the one around which we revolve. In astronomy, it has a name. The name is Sol. It is called Sol because it is *alone*, because it is solitary. This is the fate of a star. Whether human or celestial, a star has a lonely existence.

BEING A HOST OR HOSTESS

Stop Playing the Role of Popular Host or Hostess. Perhaps you pride yourself on entertaining a lot of people,

on cooking exceptionally good meals, on opening your home to others. These can be all be wonderful things to do—up to a certain limit. Diana L. was a popular hostess. She frequently slaved all day making a dinner for her friends and even for acquaintances. One day, exhausted, she asked herself, "Why am I doing this?" She realized that only a few of the people she entertained so royally ever invited her back. In the case of one couple, she realized that she had given them ten dinners and she had been invited to their house only once!

Diana talked the situation over with her husband, and they both agreed that they would entertain only people who reciprocated in an appropriate manner. She says, "When I made this decision, I felt like a workhorse that had its harness removed. I'm experiencing so much relief! I see now that I was, in a way, trying to buy friendship. Entertaining can, under certain circumstances, be a joyful, gratifying experience. But it can also be a disenchanting, demoralizing one. When it finally dawned on me that I felt more used and abused than gratified, I quit playing the role of popular hostess. I still entertain, of course, but selectively."

CLUBS AND ORGANIZATIONS

If You Are a Member of More Than Three Clubs or Organizations, Reduce the Total Number to Two. Memberships in clubs and organizations can be an effective way to cope with loneliness, up to a point. But if you belong to more than two organizations, you will often find that there are just too many demands on your time. Elise F. was a member of the PTA, a club affiliated with the local YWCA, and a bridge club. She and her husband also belonged to a square dancing club. She was often out of the house four nights a week and members of the square dancing club sometimes pressured the couple to go on weekend excursions. She served as secretary of the PTA and had to both take and report minutes. She was in charge of finding speakers for the club affiliated with the YWCA. She and her husband were on the square dancing club's entertainment committee.

Elise says, "I was wearing myself out. I felt frazzled and tense. A lot of what was supposed to be fun had become a series of *musts*. I wanted to have a lot of friends and be well liked. But I realized that I was running myself ragged for nothing. There was no point to it. I was so popular that I didn't have time for anybody. Right now I belong only to the PTA and the square dancing club. And I feel a lot better. I've got some time for *me*."

INTROVERSION

If You Are a Natural Introvert, Look Upon the Idea of Popularity as Somewhat Offensive to Your Nature. The idea of popularity is a peculiarly twentieth-century idea associated primarily with the United States. For example, a hundred years ago people in towns and villages in England didn't worry about being popular. They were much more likely to be individuals, to be a bit eccentric. Read novels by Jane Austen, Thomas Hardy, or Charles Dickens and you will see what I mean. Oh, of course people knew people and had friends. But they didn't, in general, place a high premium on being popular.

These observations are particularly important if you are a natural introvert, a person who needs a substantial amount of time with yourself in order to think, carry out projects, or just get away for a while. If you tend to be introverted, this doesn't mean that you don't like or need people. However, it *does* mean that you need spaces between your interactions with others. And it also means that for a person like you popularity is a false and unimportant goal. Don't think that you *ought* to be popular, that it is something you *should* be. There is no ought or should about it. Do what you *want* to do in this regard. There is no moral principle that says popularity is an intrinsic human value.

If you are a natural introvert, being popular can make you feel *more*, not less, lonely. Forcing yourself to have a lot of superficial contacts can be counterproductive.

POPULARITY AND A PARTNER

Understand That If You Seek Popularity, You Are Likely to Induce Loneliness in a Partner. Let's assume that you are married. As you become more and more popular, you may begin to neglect your spouse. Drake M. was a businessman in a small town. He belonged to many clubs and organizations, devoted himself to civic affairs, and played golf every Saturday. His wife, a traditional woman, stayed with him for a variety of reasons. But she became obese and felt sorry for herself. She was a very lonely woman, and experienced herself as cast aside by her popular husband.

Al Jolson was one of the biggest singing stars of the century. He played the lead in the first full-length talking motion picture, *The Jazz Singer*. His film biography, *The Jolson Story*, portrays a married couple, Jolson and the dancer Ruby Keeler, very much in love. However, Jolson was addicted to his fame and the admiration of the crowd. Toward the end of the film, Keeler leaves him because she recognizes that he is too egocentric to offer her the kind of nurturing love that we all need.

The ironic part of all of this is that the one who seeks popularity is also lonely. Drake is popular, but emotionally disconnected from his partner. By all accounts, Al Jolson was a very lonely man. The cost of popularity can be very high.

ILLUSION

Look Upon the Idea That Popularity Is Important as an Illusion. A basic teaching in Eastern wisdom is that the world we perceive is *maya*, or illusion. The central notion is that we often act as if we are bewitched, and we behave like people in a dream. Much of what we take to be real is based on false assumptions and poor logic. If we treat the perceived world of maya as reality, we often do many foolish things.

The idea that popularity is important can be looked upon as an aspect of maya. This chapter has revealed in a number of ways how the attachment to popularity is useless, can backfire, and can aggravate loneliness. The next time you find yourself drawn to behaviors geared to make you popular, ask yourself, "Am I overdoing it? Am I selling my individuality for the pottage of popularity? Am I spellbound by a cultural illusion?" The answers that naturally occur to you may set you free from the illusion cast by the idea of the importance of popularity.

A FEW RELATIONSHIPS

Seek a Few Deep Relationships, Not a Multitude of Superficial Ones. It is, of course, a good idea to have more than one friend. And, ideally, you should have close relationships with a partner, children, and your larger

family. But you don't need a multitude of superficial relationships. Again, you don't *need* to be what in our culture we call "popular."

Close relationships should have some depth to them.
What is meant by a "deep" relationship? It is one characterized by either common interests or common values, or
both. Sometimes it is not possible to have both. For example, your relationships with brothers, cousins, and so
forth may be based more on commonly shared values
than on common interests. A mutually held sense of the
meaning of life, the importance of duty, and of attitudes
in general, give you a common ground for a relationship.
These are relationships that have what we call "heart."
They satisfy emotional needs, not cognitive ones.

On the other hand, friendships may focus more on
common interests. And these *will* satisfy cognitive needs,
needs associated with curiosity and mental stimulation.
If, for example, you have an interest in a subject such as
music, novels, cooking, travel, playing bridge, arranging
flowers, investing in stocks, or sports, seek out people
with similar interests.

I still remember when I arrived on the UCLA campus
as a junior. I was twenty years old, and knew no one. One
of my first friends was Donovan G. In our first conversation we both discovered that we had read a book called
Why Write a Novel by Jack Woodford. We were both big
fans of the book, wanted to write, and so forth. This common interest formed the first cement for a friendship that
lasted for many years. My friendship with Donovan
helped me overcome an initial sense of great loneliness as
I tried to become oriented to a large college campus.

The Last Word

The person who compulsively seeks popularity is a study
in dissatisfaction. Popularity cannot really address the
problem of loneliness. And popularity cannot be sustained. The author Paul Chatfield said, "Popularity is like

the brightness of a falling star, the fleeting splendor of a rainbow, the bubble that is sure to burst by its very inflation."

Key Points to Remember

◻⟶ It is common for lonely persons to think that a possible antidote to their negative state is to achieve a state of greater popularity.

◻⟶ Develop a deeper understanding of the word *popular.*

◻⟶ Remember that you can't please everyone.

◻⟶ Reject the idea that you need to be liked by everyone.

◻⟶ Don't envy popular people their social stardom.

◻⟶ Stop playing the role of popular host or hostess.

◻⟶ If you are a member of more than three clubs or organizations, reduce the number to two.

◻⟶ If you are a natural introvert, look upon the idea of popularity as somewhat offensive to your nature.

◻⟶ Understand that if you seek popularity, you are likely to induce loneliness in a partner.

◻⟶ Look upon the idea that popularity is important as an illusion.

◻⟶ Seek a few deep relationships, not a multitude of superficial ones.

7 AGGRESSIVENESS AND EMOTIONAL ISOLATION: THE TOP DOG IS A SOLITARY DOG

You know people who *have to* win.

Maybe you are even one of them.

This chapter is about winning, aggressiveness, manipulation, and how these factors play a significant role in loneliness.

The novel *What Makes Sammy Run?* by Budd Schulberg tells the story of a young man named Sammy Glick who uses and abuses people, passes himself off as a creative writer by stealing another man's screenplay, lies, cons, cheats, and finally makes it to the top as a motion picture producer. He will step on anyone who gets in his way. He has no genuine feeling, no heart. He is an I-want-mine machine in human form.

Toward the end of the novel he has "everything." He is making big money, he has power and status, and he marries a beautiful Hollywood starlet. Shortly after his marriage he finds her in bed with another man. He realizes that he has *nothing*, that all of his striving and ambition has produced a big fat emotional zero. He is an empty, hollow man.

He is a *lonely* man.

The Need for Power

The psychologist Alfred Adler asserted that human beings have an inborn need for power. He adopted and adapted this idea from the writings of the philosopher Friedrich Nietzsche who said that the will to power is a great urge toward upward striving in all of us. When the need for power is in normal balance with other needs, it manifests itself as what has been called *effectance motivation*. Effectance motivation is the wish to be reasonably competent. In children, it plays a role in the desire to walk, to talk, to read and write, to assemble objects, to play with toys, to learn to ride a tricycle, and so forth. In adults we can see effectance motivation at work whenever we want to master a task, to rise to a challenge. It is normal to want to be as good as the other person, to live up to your own expectations. And underlying all of this is the need for power.

So the need for power is not "bad."

However, the need for power can become pathological. In some people, like Sammy, it appears to be excessive. The question asked in the Schulberg novel's title can be translated as follows: Why does Sammy do what he does? This question can be answered readily enough. Sammy is dominating and aggressive because he has a pathological need for power. This excessive inner push causes him to take advantage of others whenever he can. And it *also dominates him*. It is self-defeating, in the long run, for Sammy too, leading, as we have seen, to a meaningless existence and loneliness.

Top Dog and Underdog

The Gestalt therapist Frederick "Fritz" Perls used to say that the personality contains two clowns, the top dog and the underdog. Like clowns in a circus, they continually trip each other. The top dog is forceful and dominating. It must have its way, and it is always trying to defeat the underdog by aggressive tactics. The underdog is forced to accept defeat at one level, but usually gets back at the top dog indirectly, by passive-aggressive strategies or by cheating.

For example, let's say that you are overweight. It's your top dog that puts you on a diet. It says, "OK, from here on it's only 1,000 calories a day for you until you lose forty pounds." The "you" in the prior sentence is *the self*, the personality as experienced. Unfortunately, the self is able to produce another aspect, the underdog. So the underdog cheats on the diet, goes on a binge, and so forth. And nothing is accomplished.

What is true *within* the human personality is also true *between* personalities. If you are dealing with another person, both of you have potential top dogs and underdogs. If you are determined, as Sammy was, to always have your top dog run the show in your human interactions, then other people will "lose" to you. If others are captured in your field of influence, they will be forced into the underdog role. A person who is afraid to lose his or her job provides an example of someone who might feel like an underdog. Another example is provided by a person who appears to be trapped in a loveless marriage.

But the underdog will find ways to thwart the top dog's need for power. The dominated employee may make errors, work without enthusiasm, and in subtle ways sabotage the employer's goals. The dominated spouse may become withdrawn, act depressed, and lose sexual interest. Again, the top dog loses by "winning."

Loneliness will be the bitter fruit harvested by insisting on being the top dog in any significant relationship.

Coping Strategies

I don't know if you have an excessively strong tendency to dominate others. I hope you don't. But if you see yourself even half-mirrored in the description of Sammy Glick's behavior, you might think twice about your own behavior. The overexpression of the need for power can be a potent factor in inducing or aggravating loneliness.

The coping strategies presented in this section will help you temper the kinds of aggressive behaviors that promote emotional isolation.

REVISITING THE NEED FOR POWER

Recognize That a Need for Power Can Be Excessive. This suggestion reaffirms what has already been stated. But it bears repeating. The need for power is inborn and natural. If in balance with other needs and drives, it is normal. However, if it gets out of hand, it can become self-defeating and pathological.

Henry O. has been married to Opal for twelve years. Throughout their marriage Henry has been top dog. Opal began seeing a clinical psychologist with the complaint that she was depressed. Henry's reaction was, "She hasn't got anything to be depressed about. She has a good car, a beautiful home, two healthy children, and plenty of spending money. It must be biological—probably the chemical messengers in her brain or some such thing."

The psychologist asked Opal to bring Henry to one of the sessions, and after being asked three weeks in a row, Henry grudgingly complied. Fortunately, the psychologist was both skilled and caring, and he was able to establish a supportive relationship with Henry. Little by little, Henry grew to see that he had been overly dominating. He made all of the important decisions in the household, treated his wife like a child, and discounted her opinions. Much of her depression was linked to repressed rage.

In time Henry recognized that his need for power was excessive, and that his wife wasn't the only one who was suffering in the relationship. He had been denying that he was lonely, but he was finally able to face his loneliness. As Henry discovered ways to modify his excessive need for power, Opal began to feel less depressed. As she became more nurturing and affectionate, he began to feel less lonely.

ASSERTIVENESS AND AGGRESSIVENESS

Be Assertive, Not Aggressive. When aggressive persons with a high need for power are told that it would be a good idea to back off a bit, they are threatened. Giving up an aggressive style is perceived as a loss of control. And they certainly don't want to flip positions and become passive underdogs.

Fortunately, a hard choice doesn't have to be made. One is not confronted with the extremes of aggressiveness at one end of the pole and passive acceptance at the other end. There is a happy medium. It is called *assertiveness*. Assertive behavior is neither passive nor aggressive. It is the "just right" social response between two extremes.

When you are assertive, you (1) stand up for your rights, (2) don't allow yourself to be manipulated, (3) speak firmly and with conviction, (4) have positive regard for the other person, and (5) avoid venting arbitrary hostility.

If you have a tendency to be overly aggressive in your human interactions, make an effort to replace aggressiveness with assertiveness. You will be pleased with the result.

MANIPULATION

Don't Manipulate. Manipulation is a form of hidden aggression. Human beings manipulate when they either want to mask their hostility or they believe that they are in too weak a position to use open aggressiveness. In both cases the aim of manipulative behavior remains the same: The person pulling strings is trying to get his or her way and attain a top dog position.

Think about the movie *Robin Hood* or other films presenting a portrayal of court intrigue. The reigning monarch, king or queen, is never portrayed as a manipulator. He or she has too much power. But the first minister or other lieutenant of the monarch *is* presented as a con artist. The reason for this is that the minister is in a weaker position and *must* manipulate in order to attain his goals.

Take note of the fact that the manipulative individual is almost always presented as a villain. Iago, who manipulated Othello into murdering his beloved Desdemona, is another example of a trusted officer who abused his position.

If in a significant relationship such as a marriage or a friendship, you manipulate in order to get your way, you will eventually be perceived as a kind of villain. The other person will grow to detest you. You will drive the other individual away, and this will worsen your loneliness.

You may feel that your manipulative behavior is justified because you want to maintain the facade of love or affection. Or you may feel that it is justified because you are taken for granted. But manipulation is never justified because its eventual emotional cost to you, as well as to others, will be too high.

USING OPEN ANGER

Refrain From Using Open Anger to Get Your Way. If you can't get your way by manipulating, what then? Well, you might be tempted to use open anger. There are persons who snap, growl, shout, gripe, snarl, and say mean things in order to dominate. As a short-run tactic this will work *if* the other person has a large reservoir of good feeling toward you. The other individual will dip into the pool and bring out a bucket of kindness, giving in as a way of keeping the peace.

But even submissive peacemakers can reach a limit. They arrive at a point where they have gone to the well once too often and the bucket comes up empty. We then say that "the worm turns." And if you are in the habit of using open anger to get your way, you may find yourself bereft of the very affection you crave.

PERSONALITY

Don't Think of Aggressiveness as a Personality Trait. Both manipulation and open anger are types of aggressiveness. If you are prone to excessively use either tactic in your personal relationships, you may rationalize by thinking, "Well, that's just the way I am. It's a part of my personality. So I can't help it."

If you really believe that aggressiveness is a personality trait, then you can't separate it from the self. It belongs to you the way your fingers and your toes belong to you. And, of course, this helps to make your behavior self-justifying.

But notice that I used the word *rationalize* in the first paragraph. A rationalization is an ego defense mechanism. It is one of the ways in which we baby the ego and maintain self-esteem. A rationalization is an *excuse* for irresponsible behavior. Confront your own rationalizations. In this case, say to yourself, "Aggressive behavior is something I *do*. It is *not* a personality trait. I'm not locked into it. I can stand apart from it and choose to replace aggressiveness with assertiveness."

If you keep rationalizing that you can't help your aggressiveness, then this will add one more stone to the pathway leading toward emotional isolation.

SIBLING RIVALRY

Think in Terms of Sibling Cooperation, Not Sibling Rivalry. Alfred Adler had much to say about the will to power and how it sometimes created problems in families. He was one of the first psychologists to focus on the importance of such factors as birth order and sibling rivalry. He noted that a first-born child is often openly hostile toward a second-born child. This is particularly true if the first born is a toddler or a preschooler when the second one arrives. The first child feels *dethroned*, knocked out of his or her top dog status. For example, an older child who has already been toilet trained may regress and start eliminating in an inappropriate manner again. The obvious, and correct, psychological interpretation is that he or she is trying to get the affection and attention that the infant is getting.

The years pass, the children grow, and sibling rivalry often continues. As we have seen, the older child is constantly striving to either maintain or regain a top dog status. But what about the younger child? He or she feels like an underdog for various reasons. The older child seems smarter and more competent. (This is only because he or she has a greater chronological age; but the younger child doesn't understand this.)

The younger sibling often operates on this principle: "If you're number two, you've got to try harder." The struggle often continues through adolescence into adulthood.

Note that sibling rivalry has its roots in early childhood. The very words *sibling rivalry* suggest immature behavior. Adults who are competing with each other like the children they once were should stop and reflect and think twice about what they are doing. It is prudent to think, "Sibling rivalry is kid stuff."

Dominique F. is thirty-three years old and two years younger than her older sister, Elaine. Dominque says, "My sister and I have always had an excessive rivalry with each other. We've been jealous of each other's boyfriends, husbands, clothes, and careers. I know this is horrible, but it's almost as if I haven't been able to be content if Elaine wasn't failing in some way. And I think she's felt the same way.

"But I know we love each other. Our competitive natures have driven us apart, and we are lonely for each other, for what we might have together. One of us has to take the first step to simply stop the silly game we've been playing. And I'm not going to wait for Dominique. I'm going to take responsibility for my own behavior and start thinking of ways I can go *with* Elaine down life's lane instead of thinking of ways I can go *against* her."

Adult siblings are not like children. They no longer *need* to antagonize each other the way they once did when they were too young to know better. Cooperation is the rational replacement for rivalry.

WIN-WIN SOLUTIONS

Think in Terms of Win-Win Solutions, Not in Terms of Win-Lose Patterns. When an individual has an excessive need for power, he or she automatically thinks of human relationships in win-lose terms. Mallory wants to go see an action-adventure movie tonight. His wife, Eugenia, wants to go see a romantic comedy. Mallory, insisting on being the top dog, becomes loud and belligerent, pushing hard to get his way. They go see the action-adventure movie, and on the way he is thinking, "Good. I won."

But that evening Eugenia is strangely unresponsive to his sexual advances. She is quiet and withdrawn. Mallory is frustrated and feels "out in the cold." His "I win" has turned sour. It has become a loss instead of a gain.

How could he have approached the movie-going situation in win-win terms? He should have negotiated with Eugenia, made a little contract. He will go see a romantic comedy with her if she will go see an action-adventure movie with him. This would have allowed them both to feel gratified. Neither of them would have felt discounted. This is the kind of win-win solution that human beings need to seek.

SCAPEGOATING

Be Aware of the Tendency to Scapegoat Aggression. Let us say that you had a bad day at work. You come home and take out your pent-up hostility on your partner. This very natural tendency is a process known as *scapegoating aggression.* Yolanda G. says, "I'm a waitress in a family restaurant. My style is to be warm and cheerful and helpful to all customers, even those who treat me more like a robot than a human being. The other day I came home mad, really mad. I felt that I had been abused by just one customer too many. If felt that a martyr. I began giving my husband, Phil, a very hard time about two or three things that I didn't like about his behavior and attitude.

"Finally, Phil said, 'Look, honey. I know you've had a bad day. But don't take it out on me.'

"His comment drew me up short. And I realized that I really *was* taking it out on him. I could also see that if I kept this kind of thing up it would place a wall between us. Now when I have a bad day I try to think of other ways to release my hostility instead of dumping on my husband."

FUTILITY

Recognize the Ultimate Futility of the Exercise of Power.
The raw use of power in human relationships will bring about exactly what you *don't* want: an aggravation of your sense of loneliness.

The poem *Ozymandias*, written about 175 years ago by Percy Bysshe Shelley, clearly communicates the general futility associated with the exercise of power. It is presented below in its entirety:

> *I met a traveller from an antique land*
> *Who said: "Two vast and trunkless legs of*
>   *stone*
> *Stand in the desert. Near them, on the sand,*
> *Half sunk, a shattered visage lies, whose*
>   *frown,*
> *And wrinkled lip, and sneer of cold*
>   *command,*
> *Tell that its sculptor well those passions read*
> *Which yet survive, stamped on these lifeless*
>   *things,*
> *The hand that mocked them and the heart*
>   *that fed;*
> *And on the pedestal these words appear:*
> *'My name is Ozymandias, king of kings;*
> *Look on my works, ye Mighty, and despair!'*
> *Nothing beside remains. Round the decay*
> *Of that colossal wreck, boundless and bare*
> *The lone and level sands stretch far away."*

The Last Word

In significant relationships—those involving friends and family—there is no place for the exercise of raw power. If you have adopted an authoritarian style in your personal

dealings, one characterized by a tendency to be overcontrolling, think twice about what you are doing. You may get what you want in the short run. But in the long run, you will have to pay a price. And that price is an intensified feeling of loneliness.

Key Points to Remember

⊶ Both the psychologist Alfred Adler and the philosopher Friedrich Nietzsche asserted that human beings have an inborn need for power.

⊶ The need for power can become pathological.

⊶ According to the Gestalt therapist Frederick "Fritz" Perls, the personality contains two clowns, the top dog and the underdog.

⊶ Recognize that a need for power can be excessive.

⊶ Be assertive, not aggressive.

⊶ Don't manipulate.

⊶ Refrain from using open anger to get your way.

⊶ Don't think of aggressiveness as a personality trait.

⊶ Think in terms of sibling cooperation, not sibling rivalry.

⊶ Think in terms of win-win solutions, not in terms of win-lose patterns.

⊶ Be aware of the tendency to scapegoat aggression.

⊶ Recognize the ultimate futility of the exercise of power.

8 WHEN MALE MEETS FEMALE: FALLING IN LOVE WITH LOVE

Here is an excerpt from the journal of Edith L., a thirty-three-year-old high school English teacher:

> It's two o'clock in the morning and I've just finished watching an old movie on the Golden Classics channel. It was Tarzan and his Mate with Johnny Weissmuller and Maureen O'Sullivan. The host said it was made in 1934. I got an instant crush on Weissmuller when he told O'Sullivan in no uncertain terms, "Me Tarzan! You Jane!" There was no mistaking his intentions. He wanted her. And he was making a commitment to her.
>
> I enjoyed the movie, but now I feel in low spirits. I've gone through one too many rotten relationships. Where is my Tarzan? Doesn't anybody want me to be his Jane?
>
> Why do I and a guy start out with a bang and end up with a fizzle? There's got to be a better way.

Edith is putting a common frustration into words. It is not at all unusual for a man and a woman to meet, to be attracted, to find each other exciting, only to be rewarded in the long run with the ashes of a burned-out romance.

It is an old, old story. In its most tragic form it is the basic plot line of two great novels, *Anna Karenina* by Leo Tolstoy and *Madame Bovary* by Gustave Flaubert. In the

hands of commercial writers, it is a tale that has been told countless times in "true confession" magazines. There are many, many versions of the story. But the basic elements are these:

1. A male and female meet.

2. There is great sexual attraction.

3. One, or both, of the partners believes that there is a basis for a sincere, long-term relationship.

4. There is sexual involvement. However, there is lack of complete emotional commitment on the part of at least one of the individuals.

5. For various reasons, the worm of dissatisfaction eats away at the couple's pleasure in each other. (The "various reasons" will be explored later.)

6. They part—often with tears and rancor.

7. One, or both, feels rejected, used, and lonely.

As Edith comments in her journal, "There's got to be a better way."

Fortunately, there *is* a better way. The skills and techniques pointing to that better way are presented in this chapter. They will give you insight into the process of male-female attraction. More than that, they will make it possible for you to *nurture* that process, to lift it to its fullest potential.

Coping Strategies

Nurturing a relationship is a matter of making the right moves at the right time. As in a game of chess, everything depends on *strategies*. This *does not* mean you have to manipulate and "be clever." On the contrary, this is one of the *worst* strategies that you can follow. As indicated in Chapter 7, manipulation drives people away. It destroys intimacy. It aggravates loneliness.

The coping strategies to be presented are based on the real, not the imaginary, needs of a romantic relationship. As a consequence, they will appeal to your rational self. And you will see that they have direct and immediate applied value.

THE IFD SYNDROME

Understand the IFD Syndrome. Your first task is to comprehend a general pattern that cuts away at the quality of many relationships. This pattern is called the *IFD syndrome*, and it was first presented some years ago in the

book *People in Quandaries* by Wendell Johnson. Johnson, an expert in communication theory, was interested in how the use of language affects thought and emotion.

The capital letters *IFD* stand for idealization, frustration, and demoralization. *Idealization* is a mental-emotional process that takes place in the first phase of a relationship. If you are prone to idealization, then you describe the other person in glowing terms. You may actually use the words out loud when talking to friends. Or you may think about the person. Cognitive psychology suggests that we usually think in words. One way to define thinking is to say that it is the sentences we run through our conscious minds. Here are a few examples of statements, said to others or the self, that reflect idealization:

1. He's wonderful! Just the greatest guy I've ever met.

2. She's perfect! Where has she been all my life?

3. He's so good looking. He could be a movie star.

4. She's so beautiful. She could win a beauty contest.

5. He's the most intelligent man I've ever met.

6. She's the most charming woman I've ever met.

7. He's just wonderful with children. He would make a great father.

It would be possible to go on and on. But you get the idea. The tendency to idealize is very strong. Why do we do it? There are a number of reasons, but three will be identified. First, we idealize because we are subconsciously programmed to do so from early childhood. Fairy tales such as "Snow White" and "Cinderella" suggest that all of our problems will be solved when we meet the right person. And the right person will be *perfect for us*.

Second, we idealize because the human mind has a natural tendency to make projections. We automatically impose our needs and wishes on a person who might be able to fulfill them. The person is not seen as he or she really is, but as we want him or her to be. Projection induces us to form unrealistic expectations about the other person.

Third, we want the best for ourselves. We *hope*. And this hope gets translated into an idealization about *this* person. You begin to think that for sure this time you've met Mr. Right or Ms. Perfect.

Frustration takes place in the second phase of a relationship. The other person is not the person you thought he or she was. You are disappointed. Your disappointment arises from the fact that you had idealized. When the other individual fails to live up to the unrealistic expectations that you have imposed on him or her, you feel frustrated. You see this as the other person's fault. You may not analyze the situation and see that the other individual never made a contract to act the way you wanted him or her to act. You feel blocked. The relationship begins to get rocky.

Demoralization takes place in the third and last phase of a relationship. You have lost all hope. You and the other person have finally broken off. He or she was no good at all. It was all a big mistake. You feel spiritless and helpless. You wonder if you will ever be able to establish a long-term affectionate relationship with anybody. This demoralization phase can last quite a long time. And during this phase you are very lonely.

AVOIDING IDEALIZATION

Avoid Idealization. It is not enough to be aware of the IFD syndrome. You've got to *do* something about it. What? Most of the problem is associated with the first phase: idealization. Idealization is a cognitive error. It is a mental distortion. It places an artificial warp on the whole relationship from the very beginning. If you idealize another individual, you have already set yourself up for your own emotional fall. It is important to say to yourself from the start such statements as:

"Remember, nobody's perfect."

"OK. Expect a lot. But don't expect *everything*."

"There's bound to be a few surprises. A person puts his or her best foot forward at the beginning. I've got to wait a while to find out who this person *really* is."

"Don't get too excited. Calm down."

If you begin a relationship with realistic, not unrealistic, expectations, you protect yourself against the two subsequent phases of frustration and demoralization.

Giselle D., a woman with a history of disappointing relationships, says, "Now when the love bug bites, the first thing I think is, 'Watch out for the old IFD syndrome.' And the first thing that I do is to avoid idealization."

IDENTITY AND EMOTIONAL CLOSENESS

Establish an Identity Before You Attempt to Establish Emotional Closeness. One of the chief characteristics of a stable long-term relationship is emotional closeness. *Emotional closeness* between two people exists when they enjoy each other's company, when they share common values and interests, when they find themselves attracted to each other as persons, and when they have genuine respect for each other.

According to Erik Erikson, a leading investigator into developmental theories of personality, the formation of an identity takes place in adolescence. He designates the challenge of forming an identity as the fifth stage of psychosocial development. *Psychosocial development* refers to the development of the personality in the framework of its interactions with other people.

You have an *identity* when you know who you really are, when you have a robust sense of self, and have a strong sense of direction in life. In theory, an identity should be relatively well formed toward the end of adolescence, around the age of eighteen. Unfortunately, research in social psychology suggests that today many people have a difficult time attaining a sense of identity. Often they are still trying to bring it into focus when they are in their mid-twenties.

If your identity is not well defined, then it will be hard for you to make a mature commitment to another person.

You will still be too self-absorbed and concerned with your own emotional needs to take a real interest in the other person's psychological world.

An alternative possibility is that your own identity *is* well defined, but you have met a person who is still struggling to find one. Perhaps you want to play the social role of "Rescuer." You have the fantasy that your concern and affection will be enough to make your relationship work. You will probably be wrong. If the other person can't meet your emotional needs in the same way that you are meeting his or hers, there is very little basis for emotional closeness.

Rachel H. is a twenty-three-year-old bank teller, and she sometimes takes classes in the evening at a local community college. She says, "I met Davis about two years ago in a class in music appreciation. He told me he had a dream—he was going to be a successful songwriter. He related lengthy anecdotes about Harry Warren and Irving Berlin. He was so intense and interesting and spellbinding that I began to share his dream. I was willing to chuck everything for him. I made a foolish commitment to him without really evaluating who he was.

"We became sexually involved within only a few weeks of meeting each other. About three months into the relationship he notified me that he was giving up songwriting. Publishers didn't know talent when they saw it. He had just finished reading a book called *How I Raised Myself From Failure to Success in Selling* by Frank Bettger, and he was going to make a quick fortune selling life insurance just the way Bettger did.

"It was hard for me to make a readjustment, but I wanted to be supportive to my man. So, little by little, I bought into the make-a-lot-of-money-fast selling insurance notion. Actually, Davis did pretty well in insurance sales. He was top man with his company three months in a row. By now we were living together. And then one day he pulled the rug out from under me again and announced that he wanted to go to college full time and eventually become a medical doctor. He had the idea that

I could work and support us both while he went to school.

"I felt as if I had been socked in the stomach. I took a good long look at what was going on, and realized that I was doing all of the giving. He was charming and superficially affectionate. But he was an emotional parasite. Fortunately I found enough strength to break it off with Davis. But I regret ever getting involved with him. I wasted time on a person who was too emotionally immature to really build anything enduring with."

So, before you expect to form a real and lasting bond with another person, ask yourself these questions: Do I have a fairly well-defined identity? Does the other person appear to me to have formed a strong sense of identity? If the answer to either question is no, then proceed with caution. The foundation for an enduring relationship does not appear to be in place.

THE HORSE AND THE CART

Put the Emotional Horse Before the Sexual Cart. The familiar saying "Don't put the cart before the horse" is readily applicable to male-female relationships. It is unfortunately true that when sparks fly and a relationship is in its exciting first stages, it is tempting to act out sexual impulses.

Aside from the very real risks of sexually transmitted diseases and unwanted pregnancies, there are other, psychological, drawbacks of premature sexual activity.

If sexual activity is premature, it is not nurtured by emotional roots. The excitement wears off, one or both of the individuals thinks that sex is all that there is to the relationship, and they begin to pull apart from each other before they have even gotten to know each other. The basic principle to remember is this: Early sexual activity does not serve the long-run interests of a relationship.

In some cases sexual involvement without a solid emotional foundation tends to induce sexual problems.

A woman may experience lack of arousal, orgasmic dysfunction, or painful intercourse. A man may experience erectile insufficiency or premature ejaculation. Disenchanted and somewhat confused, the couple lack the confidence in the relationship and the communication skills required to improve the quality of their sexual behavior. One or both of them privately decides that there is someone else out there who will be a better sexual partner. And the premature sexual activity undercuts any chance that the relationship itself has to grow.

The emotional horse should supply the energy for the relationship. It should draw the sexual cart along with it. A sexual relationship is an expression of the joy that two people take in each other's company.

PERSONS HOISTING FALSE COLORS

Beware of Persons Who Hoist False Colors. Pirates of days gone by used to sail into forbidden territorial waters by hoisting false colors, flags suggesting that they were friends. Something similar is done by persons in relationships. If a person is flying false colors, you can easily get used and abused. The other person is, in effect, a kind of pirate who takes advantage of you.

Irwin G., a forty-four-year-old divorced manager of a family restaurant, says, "When I met Katie I thought she was terrific. She was twenty-seven, divorced too, and the single mom of a three-year-old girl. Katie was fun to be with, had a lot of ideas, and was a good listener. I was letting myself fall in love a little too fast and I knew it. As the relationship quickly moved to the threshold of sexual activity, I hesitated a little. I told Katie that I didn't want to take advantage of her, that I wasn't making any promises or commitments.

"Katie laughed and told me that my reservations were old-fashioned. She was a liberated woman. Sex would be as gratifying for her as it was for me. The idea that she would be giving and I would be taking was an antiquated one associated with male chauvinism.

"So we proceeded on what I thought was an honest basis. The sex was hot and heavy for about four months, and then it began to wear off. The whole relationship began to cool down. We bickered a lot, found out that we didn't have much in common, had completely different political and religious views, and I began to draw away.

"Katie became very possessive. She wouldn't let me go. When I tried to tell her how I felt, that I wanted out, she went kind of berserk. She called me all kinds of names. She told me that I'd taken advantage of her, that I had used her. I told her that she had told me that she was a liberated woman, and this only made her angrier.

"We patched things up for a while, and I kept seeing her out of guilt. But I knew it was all wrong. When I finally decided that I had to break it off, it was even worse the second time. Finally, I was able to make the split stick, but it was very, very difficult. And I felt rotten for months afterward."

Justine L. is a thirty-four-year-old electrical engineer who has never been married. She says, "Chad wooed me in the old-fashioned way. He brought me flowers and candy, took me out to dinner, and after only a few weeks proposed marriage. I was swept off of my feet. He gave me a beautiful engagement ring and told me he adored me. When he pressed me for sexual activity, I'm afraid I gave in without much of a fight. I was enchanted.

"A few weeks later he stopped calling. When I finally got past his answering machine and in touch with him on the phone he was very cold. He said that had been in love but had now fallen out of love. That was the whole explanation. I tried to get more out of him, but he didn't even want to see me. I felt very, well, the word is *discarded*. I told him that I didn't want his lousy ring. He said that I could keep it. The next day, suspicious, I had it appraised and found out that the big 'diamond' was a cheap zircon."

≋≋ ≋≋ ≋≋ ≋≋ ≋≋ ≋≋ ≋≋ ≋≋ ≋≋

YOUR LOVE MAP

Make a Distinction Between Your Love Map and the Territory "Out There." Alfred Korzybski, author of *Science and Sanity*, was a Polish count who emigrated to the United States in the 1930s. An engineer, he founded an unusual approach to personal adjustment known as *general semantics*. General semantics, like cognitive therapy, asserts that the way we feel (an emotional state) is influenced by the way we think. In turn, the way we think is influenced by the way in which we use language. Semantics is the study of words and their meanings. Consequently, *general* semantics is the study of the widespread and extensive effects that words and their meanings have upon emotional responses and behavior. (One of the people inspired by Korzybski's viewpoint was Wendell Johnson, mentioned earlier as the first person to pinpoint the IFD syndrome.)

Korzybski argued that the way we think—using words—creates a mental map of the world. We take this map to *be* the world. This distinction is not completely original with Korzybski. Immanuel Kant, usually identified as one of the great philosophers, made a distinction between the *phenomenal world*, the psychological world of ideas in your mind, and the *noumenal world*, the actual world outside of the self. Both men noted that people tend to take the mental map, or phenomenal world, as *reality itself*. And this can have very unfortunate consequences. If the map is not a good fit with reality, it is possible to make all sorts of blunders and get into emotional trouble.

Korzybski was fond of saying, "The map is not the territory." He noted that this statement is so patently obvious that everyone ʽhas to agree with it. And, he argued, it is a sanity-making operation because it helps the individual to orient to reality.

A kind of submap of our big mental map of life and the world is our love map. The love map that you have constructed out of your childhood experiences, your culture's

teachings, fairy tales you know, the books you have read, the movies you have seen, and so forth is your guide to reality. If Korzybski and Kant are right, you even confuse it with reality.

So you have some fairly strong ideas about how things are supposed to go in a relationship, how you will be treated if you are really liked or loved, the kind of person who is physically attractive to you, what will be the right way to enjoy sex, and more. If some aspect of reality doesn't fit the expectations created by the map, you will be bitterly disappointed. You will think that there is something seriously wrong with the other person, not the ideas in your head. And you won't be motivated to change your thinking. You may make an open request that the other person change his or her ways. Or, worse, you may make a silent *unshared* demand that the other person change. And when the other person does not change, you will be angry. And you won't recognize that you're expecting him or her to be a mind reader.

You will be very unhappy if you expect the behavior of *any* other person to be a perfect fit with your love map. Unfortunately, this is *exactly* what you will expect if you don't recognize that the love map is not in and of itself the reality "out there," but only a guide to it.

It is the better part of wisdom to say to yourself, as Korzybski recommended, "The map is not the territory." It will save you from a lot of unexpected surprises and emotional upsets. And it may lead you to rewrite your love map when you need to.

SOUL MATES

Give Up the Soul Mate Theory. One of the ways in which a love map may impart a distorted impression of the social world it is intended to represent is associated with the soul mate theory. In brief, the soul mate theory says that somewhere in this world there is one person who is meant to be your lifetime partner. A celestial matchmaker has picked this person for you, and you have been picked for him or her. It is written on a particular page of the *Book of Fate* that the two of you shall meet and live happily ever after.

The idea has been presented in countless songs, movies, and other popular entertainments. For example, Arthur Freed, producer of the musical *Singing in the Rain* and author of the title song, wrote another song called "You Were Meant for Me." It indicates that the singer's beloved was fashioned in Heaven by angels and was sent to Earth strictly for the singer. More recently, the movie *Sleepless in Seattle* is based on the soul mate theory.

Against all odds, and with the help of unlikely coincidences, the Tom Hanks character and the Meg Ryan character finally connect at the end of the movie. Their mutual body language and facial expressions tell the audience that they are both thinking, "This is it!"

Don't rob yourself of the pleasure you derive from songs and movies built around the soul mate theory. Nonetheless, don't allow yourself to be subconsciously programmed by them into creating a mental love map that is an inadequate guide to reality. Say to yourself about certain popular presentations, "This is entertainment. This is cotton candy—tasty, but lacking in substance."

The primary problem with the soul mate theory is that if a relationship begins to become even a little troubled, you may think, "Well, I guess I made a big mistake getting involved. This person is obviously not the right one for me." And you will not work on a relationship, or, if you have already married, you will not make rational efforts to improve your marriage. Instead, you will be anxious to get out of the relationship in order to be in a receptive position when Mr. Right or Ms. Perfect comes along.

Many a lonely person looks back on an abandoned first relationship with regret. Erin I. says, "I got married to Logan when I was twenty-two and he was twenty-seven. He was settled, had a good, but ordinary, job, and wanted a home and family. I was restless, thought of myself as very pretty, and within three years was convinced I could have done much better than Logan. I had caught him too easily. I began to think of him as a little fish that I could throw back into the lake. Somewhere out there in the social lake was a bigger, better fish. The right fish for me. So I indicated my dissatisfaction, and, after a few ups and down, we got divorced. We had no children.

"That was over ten years ago. Since then I have dated many men, but have never married. I'm single, self-supporting, and lonely. Logan has remarried and has the family he craved. I look back with regret and tell myself that I was a little fool. But it's too late."

Don't let the soul mate theory blind you to the best qualities of a real person. *This* person, the person you see before you at a given moment, is not an ideal fashioned in paradise and sent down on a ray of sunshine just for you. Real persons have flaws. You have to make allowances and adjustments and work on a relationship with understanding and intelligence. (This is the central theme of the next chapter, on improving the quality of a marriage.)

FALLING IN LOVE WITH LOVE

Don't Fall in Love With Love. All is not fluff and puff in the songwriting world, as is clear from listening to the graphic lyrics of many of today's songs. However, even the songwriting world of almost sixty years ago sometimes oriented the listener toward reality. In 1938 Lorenz Hart and Richard Rodgers wrote a waltz called "Falling in Love with Love." The lyrics issue the warning that falling in love with love is very foolish. It is falling in love with make believe. It is juvenile and immature, not fitting of a grown-up. The concepts in this song orient you toward reality.

As Hart advises, don't fall in love with love. Don't let yourself be spellbound by the *idea* of love. Fall in love not with a notion, but with a *person*.

The Last Word

Establishing a long-term erotic relationship characterized not only by physical attraction but also by emotional closeness is one of the principal ways most of us overcome loneliness.

As you sail your ship of love into the often troubled waters of Romantic Bay, you need a reliable chart to steer

you away from the reefs and other hidden obstacles that may sink your fragile vessel. If your map is based on reality, not idealization and fantasy, you will save yourself from a lot of unnecessary suffering.

This chapter has given you the tools that will help you make a genuinely useful love map, one that will guide you safely toward the shore of emotional stability and intimacy.

Key Points to Remember

⌐⎯　　It is not at all unusual for a man and a woman to meet, to be attracted, and to find each other exciting, only to be rewarded in the long run with the ashes of a burned-out romance.

⌐⎯　　It *is* possible to nurture a relationship and lift it to its fullest potentiality.

⌐⎯　　Understand the IFD (idealization-frustration-demoralization) syndrome.

⌐⎯　　Avoid idealization.

⌐⎯　　Establish an identity before you attempt to establish emotional closeness.

⌐⎯　　Put the emotional horse before the sexual cart.

⌐⎯　　Beware of persons who hoist false colors.

⌐⎯　　Make a distinction between your love map and the territory "out there."

⌐⎯　　Give up the soul mate theory.

⌐⎯　　Don't fall in love with love.

9 THE LONELY MARRIAGE: HOW TO PARTNER

Recently I was eating dinner in a family restaurant, and from time to time I took note of the behavior of a couple who were sitting at a table not far from me. Although I had no desire to either stare or eavesdrop, they were sitting to my right and a little ahead of me. So they automatically presented themselves in a highly visible way.

They were both comfortably dressed in casual clothes, and appeared to be in their midthirties. Each was wearing a wedding ring. I assumed that they were married to each other. My assumption might have been incorrect, but I doubt it.

They seldom made eye contact and rarely smiled at each other. Neither one ever reached out and touched the other's hand for a moment as an affectionate person will sometimes do. There was virtually no conversation. Talk appeared to be limited to simple requests and questions such as, "Pass the salt," or, "Would you like another roll?" They were being polite enough to each other, but they seemed to be bored with each other's company. Most of the time they looked away from each other, out a window, at others, or down at their food.

They might as well have been sitting at separate tables. And they both appeared to be extremely lonely.

That Hideous Strength is a novel by C. S. Lewis. Chapter I presents the reflections of a woman named Jane. A significant sentence says, "In reality marriage had proved to be the door out of a world of work and comradeship and laughter and innumerable things to do, into something like solitary confinement."

It is definitely possible to be both married and lonely. The lonely marriage, one in which the husband and wife endure quite a bit of emotional distance for a prolonged period of time, is by no means uncommon.

The Institution of Marriage

The comedienne Mae West said, "Marriage is a wonderful institution. But I'm not ready for an institution yet."

It is possible to make all sort of cynical remarks about marriage. Nonetheless, it is estimated that about 92 percent of us give heterosexual marriage a try at least once in our lifetimes. Although it is true that today about 50 percent of marriages end in divorce, it is also true that on their wedding day the bride and groom are usually glowing with hope and happy anticipation.

For all of its ups and downs, marriage is still one of the primary ways in which most human beings expect to conquer loneliness. The zoologist Desmond Morris, author of *The Naked Ape*, asserts that *pair bonding*, a long affectionate attachment to one partner, is a natural, inborn-determined process in human beings. If this is correct, anything that we can do to nurture this process will be all to the good.

Coping Strategies

I am assuming in this chapter that you are already married. I am also assuming that although you love your partner and you believe that he or she loves you, the honeymoon is quite definitely over. You are either lonely or beginning to feel lonely. You sense that you and your partner are drawing apart, and you are looking for ways to stop this adverse drift from getting progressively worse.

The strategies presented below will help you cope with loneliness in marriage.

I AND THOU

Make an I-Thou Relationship Your Goal. It will help you immensely in your effort to overcome loneliness in marriage if you can clearly conceptualize what it is you really want. The theologian Martin Buber proposed that there are two basic ways in which people can relate to each other. These are the I-it relationship and the I-thou relationship.

In an *I-it relationship,* a first person sees himself or herself as an *I,* a real person with thoughts, feelings, and needs. Unfortunately, this person fails to recognize that his or her spouse is *equally human.* Consequently, the first person treats the spouse like a thing, like an object in the environment to be manipulated or used for personal gain. The spouse placed in the *it* position is seen in functional terms: He or she gets the cooking done, takes care of the kids, earns money, meets *my* sexual needs, is someone to show off to others, takes care of *me* when I'm sick, and so forth.

The spouse who is treated like an *it* feels lonely in the marriage. What is less obvious is that the egocentric spouse is also lonely. So the I-it relationship does neither partner any good, and aggravates the loneliness of both.

The movie *Casino* presents a stark portrayal of an I-it relationship. The Robert DeNiro character, the manager of a huge Las Vegas casino, marries the Sharon Stone character, a charismatic hustler. She is a self-confident free spirit and tells him that she doesn't love him. He tries to buy her with money. As the marriage progresses, he becomes increasingly controlling and dominating. Eventually she becomes a self-destructive abuser of alcohol and other drugs. Both of the individuals are portrayed as incredibly lonely. The movie is useful as a very well-drawn model of everything that a marriage should *not* be.

In an *I-thou* relationship, a first person sees himself or herself as an *I,* a real person with thoughts, feelings, and needs. However, the first person clearly recognizes that his or her partner has thoughts, feelings, and needs too. Although the first spouse wants to have his or her needs met, there is an equally great interest in meeting the needs of the other person. In a true I-thou relationship, this is not one sided. The second person reciprocates the attitude of the first person. Consequently, the I-thou relationship is based on a solid foundation of mutual concern for each other's emotional welfare.

Take this as your goal then: an I-thou relationship. Realize clearly that it *is* what you want, and this realization will help you focus your energy and behavior patterns on achieving it.

REALISTIC TERMS

See an I-Thou Relationship in Realistic Terms. There is a tendency to respond to the concept of an I-thou relationship as if it is an impossible ideal that has no factual existence. On the contrary, an I-thou relationship is grounded in the here and now, and it can be very real.

An I-thou relationship is *not* perfect. It is *not* completely free of conflict. And it has its ups and downs. On the other hand, an I-thou relationship *is* characterized by mutual respect. Although the individuals in the marriage are not in a state of steady happiness at the surface level, there *is* genuine happiness at the deep level.

It is useful in the learning process to observe the behavior of a model. (And working toward an I-thou relationship is most certainly a form of learning.) So look around you at couples you know who have been married for quite a while, who appear to really love each other, who you are convinced have made a long-term commitment to each other. And take these couples as your role models.

If there are no actual couples you know who seem to fit the bill of an I-thou relationship, you can turn to fictional portrayals. At first this might seem difficult. Sloan Wilson, author of the novels *The Man in the Grey Flannel*

Suit and *A Summer Place,* says that once he wrote a novel about a happy marriage and submitted it to many publishers. They all rejected it. The consensus was, "Who wants to read about a happy marriage?"

However, portrayals of robust marriages characterized by an I-thou relationship will not be free of surface conflict. Indeed, this is part of an important point to be made. If there *is* conflict, it will be resolved in a constructive way in a robust marriage. Although they aren't common, here are some examples of movies available on videotape that *do* provide useful depictions of I-thou relationships in marriage: *Father of the Bride; Fiddler on the Roof; Field of Dreams; I Remember Mama; Mr. Holland's Opus; Mrs. Miniver; Parenthood; Pride of the Yankees.*

THE ROLE OF DOMINATING PARENT

Don't Play the Role of Dominating Parent. One of the most tempting roles to play in a marriage is the role of dominating parent. When you identify with this role you tend to look down on your partner. Perhaps you play the role because you have a high need for power, because you want to be the top dog. Or you might play the role because you are convinced that you are much more well informed and intelligent than your partner. Or you may play the role, if you are a male, because you come from a background that stressed male superiority. Whatever your reason, *don't play the role* if you don't want to be lonely.

Even if you think that you are "right" in some abstract sense to play the role, you will find yourself being lonely. Where's your companion? You haven't got one. You've got someone you treat like a child, but not someone with whom you can really share thoughts and feelings. So playing the role of dominating parent in a marriage is self-defeating. You will lose much, much more than you gain.

≈≈≈ ≈≈≈ ≈≈≈ ≈≈≈ ≈≈≈ ≈≈≈ ≈≈≈ ≈≈≈ ≈≈≈

THE ROLE OF SUBMISSIVE CHILD

Resist Playing the Role of Submissive Child. If your partner tends to play the role of dominating parent, you may be tempted to play the role of submissive child. You may play the role for more than one reason. Perhaps you dislike conflict of any kind, and have adopted a philosophy of peace at any price. Or you may lack self-confidence. Maybe you are overly agreeable and easily manipulated into compliant postures. Perhaps you just want to be taken care of, and the child role is one without much responsibility. Whatever your reason, *don't play the role* if you don't want to be lonely.

If you allow yourself to be treated like a child, you will be discounted and not taken seriously. You won't be perceived as a companion and you won't feel like one. Your child self certainly won't want to trust self-revelations to a dominating parent. So you will be cut off from your spouse and emotionally isolated.

BEING AN ADULT

Be an Adult. If you shouldn't play the role of either a dominating parent or a submissive child, what role should you play? The answer is that you shouldn't play any role. You should *be* an adult. Be assertive with your partner, but not aggressive. When you have a problem to solve, be rational. Think in terms of the long-run welfare of the marriage, not in terms of a momentary solution.

An I-thou relationship is an adult-to-adult relationship. You communicate with each other as peers, as emotional equals. Perhaps you object that your partner tends to act in one of the two adverse modes—like a dominating parent or a submissive child. You don't want to be shadow boxing, acting like an adult all by yourself. The answer is simply this: If you *are* an adult, remember it, act accordingly, and you are likely to elicit the adult self in your partner. It may not work, but it's your best bet.

VERBAL FIGHTING

Observe the Rules of Fair Verbal Fighting. An emotionally intimate relationship is not free of conflict. It is only natural that a husband and wife will sometimes be at cross purposes and find themselves drifting into a fight. Within limits, the expression of a certain amount of aggressiveness is to be expected in a relationship. It *is* far better to be assertive than aggressive, stating a position without hostility, but with conviction. Nonetheless, research has shown that few marriages are totally free of expressions of aggression. And it has also been shown that such expressions do not necessarily lead to separation or divorce. Indeed, a *fair* fight can have the long-term effect of bringing a couple closer together.

The psychologist and marriage counselor George Bach makes a distinction between *constructive fighting* and *destructive fighting*. A destructive fight *will* drive a wedge between people. It *will* contribute to alienation from each other. It *will* aggravate the problem of loneliness in marriage. So you want to avoid destructive fighting, fighting characterized by insults, hasty generalizations, blaming, not listening to the other, and attacks on the other person's character such as, "You're lazy," "You're inconsiderate," "You're a spendthrift," "You're a cheapskate," "You're a fool," and so forth.

Here is a brief summary of the rules for constructive fighting in a marriage:

1. *Never engage in physical abuse*. No behaviors such as hitting, slapping, punching, arm twisting, and so forth are allowed.

2. *Be open about feelings*. If you feel disappointed, sad, angry, helpless, discounted, or used, bring these emotional states into the open. Put them into words. Pretending that you are not experiencing an adverse emotion is difficult, and you are not being honest with your partner. You might expect him or her to *know* how you are feeling. But he or she isn't a mind reader.

3. *Don't call the other person names*. This falls under the category of "don't attack the other person's character." But it bears repeating here. Don't call the other person a jerk, a fool, a fat slob, a dumbbell, a lousy cook, and so forth. These names hurt, and they're not even true. They're not true because they are hasty generalizations. The person who has been called a name can easily think of reasons the name is unfair.

4. *Be critical of the other person's behavior, not his or her character*. As indicated above, avoid calling the other person names. Instead, focus on his or her actions. Ask yourself, "What did my partner *do* that offends or disappoints me?" Then translate this into something specific, not general. Let's say you're on a tight budget and you believe that

your partner spends too much money on compact discs. Your partner comes home from the music store with a new compact disc. It is legitimate to say, "Another compact disc! You bought one three days ago! I wish you had waited at least a couple of weeks. I don't think we can afford to buy another one so soon." This is better than saying, "You're a spendthrift. You're wasting all of our money."

5. *Listen to the other person*. If the other person is talking, don't interrupt. Hear your spouse out. When he or she makes a natural stop, summarize briefly what he or she has said. You can even ask, "Am I getting it right?" This will make the other person feel understood and taken seriously. Also, make good eye contact. Don't look away when your spouse is talking to you.

6. *Argue about real issues*. Save your emotions for something that really counts, not something trivial. There is no sense in flying off the handle because a dish has not been washed or a tool was misplaced. Real issues revolve around such important matters as sex, money, raising children, moving because of a job opportunity, and coping with relatives.

7. *Don't try to "win" a fight*. It is destructive to try to be totally triumphant in a fight, to try to get the other person to admit that he or she was all wrong and you were completely right. Putting yourself in the dominant top-dog position will make your partner feel emotionally deflated. This can only make him or her want to withdraw from you. Instead, in constructive fighting the goal is to air grievances and to explore practical solutions to real problems. At the end of the fight, there should be no "winner" and "loser." Instead, you should both be winners because the fight has

been *constructive*, and has helped to strengthen, not weaken, your relationship.

THE FOUR HORSEMEN

Beware the "Four Horsemen of the Apocalypse." John Gottman, a psychologist associated with the University of Washington in Seattle, has conducted extensive research on factors influencing success and failure in marriage. He calls criticism, contempt, defensiveness, and withdrawal the "Four Horsemen of the Apocalypse." If you are in the habit of indulging in these self-defeating behaviors, you may eventually destroy your marriage.

Criticism involves excessive fault-finding. As noted earlier, if you feel you must be critical, criticize your partner's behavior, not his or her character. To whatever extent it is possible, avoid arbitrary censure and disapproval of what your partner says and does.

Contempt refers to treating your partner as if his or her ideas don't count. Contempt is also characterized by a lack of regard for your spouse's efforts, intelligence, creative efforts, values, goals, and interests.

Defensiveness takes place when you can give, but can't take, criticism. You deny that the other person is right. You put up a wall. You bring out all of the reasons that your spouse is wrong and you are right. You act very hurt that your spouse has dared to be critical at all.

Withdrawal is characterized by a refusal to respond in a meaningful way. You give your spouse the silent treatment, the cold shoulder, leave the room, go for a walk or a ride, or even leave for a day or two. Like a child, you pout, brood, and mope.

If you catch yourself engaging in any of the behaviors associated with the "Four Horsemen of the Apocalypse," short circuit your own actions. Tell yourself, "This is destructive. What I am doing now will have an adverse impact on my marriage. And it will be a factor contributing to my own loneliness."

The Last Word

The poet and mystic Kahlil Gibran wrote a well-known book called *The Prophet*. In it, when the wise man Almustafa speaks of marriage, one of the things he says is, "Let there be spaces in your togetherness." There is much wisdom in this remark. You and your spouse are together. But you need time to be apart. You don't possess each other and you can't be *everything* to each other.

The emotional intimacy of an I-thou relationship is the kind of intimacy that allows you to be a real person, an individual in your own right.

Key Points to Remember

□— It is possible to be both married and lonely.

□— The zoologist Desmond Morris asserts that *pair bonding*, a long affectionate attachment to one partner is a natural, inborn-determined process in human beings.

□— Make an I-thou relationship your goal.

□— See an I-thou relationship in realistic terms.

□— Don't play the role of dominating parent.

□— Resist playing the role of submissive child.

□— Be an adult.

□— Observe the rules of fair fighting: (1) never engage in physical abuse; (2) be open about feelings; (3) don't call the other person names; (4) be critical only of the other person's behavior, but not his or her character; (5) listen to the other person; (6) argue about real issues; and (7) don't try to "win" a fight.

□— Beware the "Four Horsemen of the Apocalypse." The researcher John Gottman identifies these as: criticism, contempt, defensiveness, and withdrawal.

10 A NINE-STEP ANTI-LONELINESS PROGRAM

You have read this book, and where do you stand?

I hope that you have already been applying some of its strategies. Maybe you have already been getting some good results.

On the other hand, you might be stalled. You want to get started on an anti-loneliness program, but wonder where is the best place to begin.

The aim of this chapter is to give you some useful guidelines.

Breaking Out of a Self-Made Prison

Think of yourself as a person unfairly locked in a real prison, one made out of brick and steel. If you had to, how would you break out? You would need to look for a weak spot, something you could work on. In the film *The Shawshank Redemption*, the Tim Robbins character finds a way to dig a tunnel out of his cell.

Think of loneliness as a self-made prison. But it is not a perfect prison, not even a well-made one. It has many weak spots. It offers not one, but many escape routes. As you were reading, you probably intuitively perceived which avenues were most open to you. Go back over the book and make a list of five to seven of the strategies that seem to you to be the ones you can most readily implement. The strategies are all identified clearly in the form of practical suggestions, and they appear in a distinctive typeface.

Carry the list with you and refer to it often. Try to implement one of the strategies whenever you can. Although this approach appears superficially random, it is not. On the contrary, it is really a self-selected approach subconsciously determined by your own personality and emotional needs. Allow your own individuality to help you select the best way to break out of the prison of loneliness.

A Nine-Step Program

It is possible that you feel a strong desire to conquer loneliness in a systematic manner. This section provides a long-range plan.

You can follow the order of the chapters. They were presented in a rational sequence, each flowing to some extent out of the prior one. If you attack the problem of loneliness in terms of the chapter sequence, you will be on a stable, ascending staircase out of the dungeon of loneliness.

STEP 1

Turn to chapter 2, "Meeting People." This chapter is directed to you if you believe that a large part of your loneliness problem could be solved by meeting the right person or persons. Survey the suggestions made under the heading "Making Contact." Select one that seems appropriate for you, and work on it for about a week. When you feel ready, take Step 2.

STEP 2

Turn to chapter 3, "The Need for Affection." This chapter explains how we all need affection in order to maintain a sense of well being. It discusses the importance of strokes, units of recognition, and how to get them. Look over the suggestions made under the heading "Obtaining Strokes." Select one that seems to stand out in importance. Apply it to yourself for about a week. When you feel the time is ripe, take Step 3.

STEP 3

Turn to chapter 4, "The Art of Winning Friends." This chapter presents the principal factors involved in interpersonal attraction. It asserts that the way people react to you is, to a large extent, *within your control*. Scan the suggestions under the heading "Winning Friends." Make use of a strategy that is compatible with your personality. Implement the approach for about a week. When you feel ready, take Step 4.

STEP 4

Turn to chapter 5, "The Outsider." This chapter will help you understand the nature of the problem of alienation and its relation to loneliness. Review the suggestions under the heading "Overcoming Alienation." Pick out one that you believe you can act upon. Apply the strategy for about a week. When you feel ready, take Step 5.

STEP 5

Turn to chapter 6, "Popularity Is Not the Answer." This chapter reveals how the need to be popular can aggravate loneliness. Look over the suggestions under the heading "Coping Strategies." Select one that seems particularly useful, and apply it for about one week. When you feel ready, take Step 6.

STEP 6

Turn to chapter 7, "Aggressiveness and Emotional Isolation." This chapter explains how a need to win emotional battles at all costs, aggressiveness, and manipulation backfire and increase an individual's sense of loneliness. Review the suggestions under the heading "Coping Strategies." Pick out one that you believe you can put to work, and implement it for about one week. When you feel ready, take Step 7.

STEP 7

Turn to chapter 8, "When Male Meets Female." This chapter will help you keep a promising relationship from ending before it has begun. The suggestions will help you *nurture* a romantic process. Look over the suggestions under the heading "Coping Strategies." Select one that seems to stand out for you at this moment in time. Apply it for about a week. When you feel ready, take Step 8.

STEP 8

Turn to chapter 9, "The Lonely Marriage." This chapter notes that it is definitely possible to be both married and lonely. If you are presently in the emotional state described by the chapter, then it will be of particular importance to you. Look over the suggestions under the heading "Coping Strategies." Pick out one that seems to be of immediate importance. Apply it for about one week.

STEP 9

You are ready for a time-out. Forget about the program for about a week. Allow your emotional batteries to recharge.

It has been about two months since you started putting the program into effect. Maybe the problem of loneliness has been greatly reduced in magnitude. Maybe it's not even much of a problem anymore. If this is the case, shelve the book. Go looking for it again if and when you need it.

On the other hand, it is possible you that you need to repeat the program. You aren't as lonely as you were, but you want to keep working on the problem and entrench your gains. Go back to Step I. This time you might pick out alternative strategies, making fresh inroads into the problem of loneliness.

The Last Word

You don't have to be a victim of loneliness. A state of loneliness is not something you have to endure. Whatever you do, don't just roll over and play the role of Victim. You *do* need to assert yourself and take positive action. However, with a positive mental attitude and a hopeful outlook, you will find out that you can do much to help yourself. Adapt and apply the strategies in this book to your own life, and expect good results.

Key Points to Remember

□⎯ This chapter presents two alternative approaches designed to help you conquer loneliness.

□⎯ The first alternative uses the image of breaking out of a self-made prison. Using this approach, you attack the problem of loneliness by looking for five to seven weak spots in your own defenses.

□⎯ The second alternative is systematic. It is the *nine-step program* outlined in this chapter.